THE ENDURING VISION OF
NORMAN MAILER

THE ENDURING VISION OF
NORMAN MAILER

Barry H. Leeds

Leeds, Barry H.
The Enduring Vision of Norman Mailer / Barry H. Leeds
ISBN: 1-929355-11-4
First printing

Design and Composition by Shannon Gentry
Photographs by Norris Church Mailer

Barry H. Leeds
Department of English
Central Connecticut State University
New Britain, CT 06050
(860) 832-2769

Barry H. Leeds, CSU Distinguished Professor of English at Central Connecticut State University, is author of **The Structured Vision of Norman Mailer** (NYU Press) and **Ken Kesey** (Ungar).

Published by
Pleasure Boat Studio: A Literary Press
8630 Wardwell Road
Bainbridge Island•WA 98110-1589 USA
Tel/Fax: 888.810.5308
E-mail: pleasboat@aol.com
URL: http://www.pbstudio.com

This book is for

my brother

Mark N. Leeds, M.D. (1943-1984)

my mother

Paula Stark Leeds (1916-1993)

&
my daughter

Leslie Lion Leeds (1973-1996)

Acknowledgments

M y primary debts are to my loyal research assistants, Bonnie Colleen Jacques Lewis and Shennen Flannery, whose intelligence, energy, unfailing good humor and keen editorial eyes were invaluable in the preparation of this work. I also wish to thank Central Connecticut State University for the sabbatical leave that made it possible to make substantive advances in my research, and the CSU-AAUP grants that further supported my efforts.

I am grateful to my friend and mentor, Norman Mailer, for writing these books and for permission to quote from them.

Portions of this work originally appeared in different form in *Athanor, Canadian Review of American Studies, Choice, Connecticut Review, Conversations with Norman Mailer, Essays on Raging Bull, Hartford Courant, New Hampshire College Journal, The English Record, The New Review, North Dakota Quarterly,* and *Take Two: Adapting the Contemporary American Novel to Film.*

Among the friends and colleagues who have constantly encouraged me are Anthony Piccione, Barbara Lupack, Anthony Cannella, Richard Bonaccorso and Christine Doyle. My editor, Jack Estes, and my Mailerian conscience, Michael Lennon, deserve special gratitude. Thanks again for the good words and deeds, the literate advice and the shared food and drink. Most of all to Beth, who knows what she means to me.

Contents

CHRONOLOGY

1923
Born January 31, Long Branch, New Jersey,
first child and only son of
Isaac Barnett and Fanny (Schneider) Mailer.

1927
Family moves to Brooklyn, Eastern Parkway section.
Barbara Jane, Mailer's sister, born.

1939
Graduates from Boys High School, Brooklyn, New York.
Enters Harvard to study engineering.

1941
Writes "The Greatest Thing in the World," which is
published in the *Harvard Advocate*.
Mailer wins first prize in *Story*
magazine's annual college contest.

1943
Graduates from Harvard with an S.B. degree
in engineering sciences (with honors).
Writes *A Transit to Narcissus*, unpublished until
appearing in 1978 in a facsimile edition.

1944
Drafted into U.S. Army. Serves as rifleman with 112th Cavalry
Regimental Combat Team out of San Antonio, Texas. Foreign
service for eighteen months in Philippines and Japan.
Marries Beatrice Silverman.
Cross-Section prints novella, "A Calculus at Heaven."

1946
Discharged from the Army in May.
Begins *The Naked and the Dead*,
which he completes in fifteen months.
("I had lived like a mole, writing and rewriting
seven hundred pages in those fifteen months"
[*Advertisements for Myself* 93-94]).

1947
Studies at the Sorbonne under the GI Bill.

1948
The Naked and the Dead.
Campaigns for the Progressive Party's
presidential candidate, Henry Wallace.
Speaks on academic freedom for the National Council of the
Arts, Sciences and Professions.

1949
Original screenplay rejected by Samuel Goldwyn.
Begins a novel about labor unions, but drops it.
Gives a speech at the Waldorf Peace Conference.
Breaks with Progressive Party.
First child, Susan, is born.

1951
Barbary Shore.
Divorced from Beatrice Silverman.

1953
Contributing editor to *Dissent.*

1954
Marries Adele Morales.
Manuscript of *The Deer Park* accepted by G.P. Putnam after
dispute with Rinehart and rejection by six other publishers.

1955
The Deer Park.
Co-founds *The Village Voice* with
Daniel Wolf and Edwin Fancher.

1956
Writes a column for *The Village Voice* from January to May.
The Man Who Studied Yoga published in *New Short Novels* 2.

1957
"The White Negro" published in *Dissent.*
Published in book form in 1958 by CityLights Books.
"The White Negro" is most readily accessible in

Advertisements for Myself and *The Time of Our Time*.
Second child, Danielle, is born.

1959
Advertisements for Myself.
Birth of third child, Elizabeth Anne.

1960
National Institute of Arts and Letters Grant in Literature.
Stabs Adele Morales with a penknife.

1962
Deaths for the Ladies (and other disasters) published.
Begins "The Big Bite," a monthly column for *Esquire*
(November 1962–December 1963).
Begins "Responses and Reactions," a bi-monthly column for
Commentary (December 1962–December 1963).
Divorced from Adele Morales.
Marries Lady Jean Campbell.
Fourth child, Kate, is born.

1963
The Presidential Papers.
Divorced from Lady Jean Campbell.
Marries Beverly Bentley.

1964
Birth of fifth child, Michael Burks.
An American Dream appears in serial form in
Esquire (January - August).

1965
An American Dream. allegorical level
Speaks at Berkeley on Vietnam Day. (main charac.)

1966
Cannibals and Christians.
Sixth child, Stephen McLeod, is born.

1967
Why Are We in Vietnam?
The Deer Park: A Play (adapted by Mailer for the stage). This

play ran for 127 performances in an off-Broadway production
at the Theatre de Lys, New York, beginning January 31 and
closing May 21.
*The Bullfight: A Photographic Narrative
with Text by Norman Mailer.*
The Short Fiction of Norman Mailer.
Wild 90, first movie, filmed and released.
Films *Beyond the Law*.
Arrested while participating in the October
antiwar march on Pentagon; released
after being sentenced to thirty days,
twenty-five of which were suspended.
Elected to the National Institute of Arts and Letters.

1968
The Armies of the Night.
Miami and the Siege of Chicago.
*The Idol and the Octopus:
Political Writings on the Kennedy and Johnson
Administrations.*
Beyond the Law is released.
Harper's prints "The Steps of the Pentagon," the first part of
The Armies of the Night.
Mailer covers both the Democratic and Republican
conventions for *Harper's*.
Third movie, *Maidstone*, is filmed.

1969
National Book Award in Arts and Letters for
The Armies of the Night.
Pulitzer Prize in general nonfiction for *The Armies of the Night.*
Polk award for *The Armies of the Night.*
Awarded honorary Doctor of Letters by Rutgers University.
Runs on a secessionist ticket for New York Democratic mayoral
nomination with Jimmy Breslin as running mate;
campaign is unsuccessful.
Covers the Apollo 11 moon flight for *Life*.

1970
Separated from Beverly Bentley.
Appeals 1967 disorderly conduct conviction to the Supreme
Court; serves last two remaining days of his sentence.

1971
Of a Fire on the Moon.
The Prisoner of Sex.
King of the Hill.
Maidstone is released, and later published as a paperback book
with an introduction by Mailer and several essays on filmmaking.
A reading performance of one-act play titled
D.J. based on *Why Are We in Vietnam?*
is given in New York at a benefit for the
People's Coalition for Peace and Justice.
Birth of seventh child, Maggie Alexandra, to Carol Stevens.

1972
Existential Errands.
St. George and the Godfather.

1973
Marilyn: A Biography.
Awarded the MacDowell Colony Medal.

1974
The Faith of Graffiti.
An adaptation of *Barbary Shore*, written and directed by Jack
Gelber, opens in New York at the Public Theatre
and runs for eighteen days.
Signs with Little, Brown to write a
multivolume work for one million dollars.

1975
The Fight.

1976
Genius and Lust: A Journey through the
Major Writings of Henry Miller.
Some Honorable Men: Political Conventions, 1960–1972.

1978
A Transit to Narcissus.
Birth of eighth child, John Buffalo, to Norris Church.

1979
The Executioner's Song.

1980
Of Women and Their Elegance.
Pulitzer Prize in fiction for *The Executioner's Song.*
Divorced from Beverly Bentley.
Marries Carol Stevens November 7; divorced November 8.
Marries Norris Church November 11.

1981
Appears in *Ragtime*, directed by Milos Forman.

1982
Pieces and Pontifications.
Writes the script for film adaptation of *The Executioner's Song.*

1983
Ancient Evenings. big book

1984
Tough Guys Don't Dance.

1985
As President of PEN, Mailer organizes the International PEN
Conference in New York City.
Elected to the American Academy of Arts and Letters.

1986
Writes "Strawhead,"
a play produced at the Actors' Studio in New York City,
starring his daughter Kate as Marilyn Monroe.

1987
Writes and directs the film adaptation of
Tough Guys Don't Dance.

1991
Harlot's Ghost.
Receives New York State Edith Wharton Citation of Merit
(named Official New York State Author).

1992
Completes book on Pablo Picasso.

1992-1993
Travels to Russia to research book on Lee Harvey Oswald,
spending a total of six months in Minsk
working on this manuscript.

1995
Oswald's Tale: An American Mystery.
Portrait of Picasso as a Young Man.
Receives honorary Doctorate of Humane Letters
from Wilkes University.

1997
The Gospel According to the Son.

1998
The Time of Our Time published on May 8, fifty years to the day
after *The Naked and the Dead.*

1999
spooky yard why R we @ war, +
modest gives ?

INTRODUCTION

No one will ever accuse Norman Mailer of moderation. Since I wrote *The Structured Vision of Norman Mailer* (1969), treating Mailer's first fifteen books, from *The Naked and the Dead* (1948) to *The Armies of the Night* (1968), he has published at least twenty more, encompassing virtually every aspect of American society and a variety of genres. After brilliantly concluding the first twenty years of his career with *Armies* and its companion piece of similar perspective, *Miami and the Siege of Chicago*, Mailer went on to publish a series of books with similar points of view during the seventies. As J. Michael Lennon perceptively remarks in *Critical Essays on Norman Mailer* (14), however, Mailer moved gradually away from himself as an autobiographical subject as in *The Prisoner of Sex* (1971) to a decade of biographical studies of other famous or notorious figures in American culture in *St. George and the Godfather* (1972), *Marilyn* (1973), *The Fight* (1975), *Genius and Lust* (1976), *Some Honorable Men* (1976), *The Executioner's Song* (1979) and *Of Women and Their Elegance* (1980). By the end of the decade, with *Executioner* and *Elegance*, Mailer had clearly and decisively removed himself from the picture. This absence of Mailer's foreground presence is almost universally recognized as one of the great strengths of the massive, Pulitzer-Prize-winning book on Gary Gilmore, which is written in the third person limited point of view, replicating the rhythms and language of its characters.

During the 1970s, Mailer was working steadily on a long-awaited and decidedly new novel, *Ancient Evenings* (1983), which I discuss in Chapter 2. It will suffice to say here that it is a massive, paradoxical work, different from anything he had ever written before, yet informed by the pervasive themes that govern all his work: power, sexuality, violence, reincarnation, cancer, and above all, existential choice. Like many of his works, it was reviewed with responses ranging from admiration to vilification.

The Structured Vision of Norman Mailer relied upon a rigidly girdling structure, treating each book chronologically by chapter. In this, the sixth decade of Mailer's career, I find predominant themes to fall so naturally into place across works that I have chosen a thematically organized structure. Because of Mailer's somewhat undeserved notoriety in relation to the women's liberation movement, I begin with his perceptions of women and heterosexual relationships, for which his works on Marilyn Monroe, *The Prisoner of Sex* (1971) and *Genius and Lust* (1976), are the richest sources. Next are his political writings and the concept of the "psychic outlaw" as expressed in his work, notably "The White Negro" (1957), and his life. Integral to the vision of the psychic outlaw is Mailer's perception of violence in American life. Chapter 3 treats the role of ritualized violence in boxing as it provides a moral paradigm in his work, both fiction and non-fiction.

Richard Poirier suggests that "Mailer's writings are best considered as one large work" (3). If, as I believe, this is true, the heart of this mega-work is indisputably *An American Dream*. My admiration for this seminal and daring novel is clear in the discussions of all of Mailer's work that follow. Chapter 4 details the parallels between *Tough Guys Don't Dance* (1984) and *American Dream*, which also tangentially inform Chapter 5, on Mailer's movies. So, too, does the massive and ambitious *Harlot's Ghost* (1991), subject of Chapter 6, look back toward *Dream* while simultaneously taking Mailer's themes a large step further, which is to say that his work is fugue-like, reworking and advancing rather than simply reiterating his sophisticated, intense and comprehensive perceptions of the human (and more particularly the American) condition.

Because of the allusions to my interview with Mailer throughout these pages, it is reproduced in its entirety as Chapter 7 for ready reference. Chapter 8 comprises a brief summary of the major books about Mailer and his work. And in response to the questions so frequently posed by students, colleagues and acquaintances ("What's he like?" and "Do you know him personally?"), I've included a summary of my admittedly limited but increasingly personal association with this fascinating artist and cultural icon, which constitutes Chapter 9, "Mailer and Me."

For reasons made clear in Chapter 9, I experienced a hiatus of a few years in my critical writings on Mailer. During that period, he published his book on Pablo Picasso and another on Lee Harvey Oswald, both during 1995. Still more impressive was his brilliant and controversial "autobiography" of Jesus Christ, *The Gospel According to the Son* (1997). And in 1998, marking his own 75th birthday and the 50th anniversary of the publication of *The Naked and the Dead*, Mailer culled from the massive body of his work to date a magnificent, weighty collection of his best work, *The Time of Our Time,* which stands as a history of the second half of the Twentieth Century as witnessed and presented by Norman Mailer. Chapter 10 treats these works with an undeserved brevity and attempts to pull together for the reader the various strands in the rich warp and woof which constitute the tapestry of the Mailer canon to date.

The best writing in the volume you hold is by Mailer himself. If I have often remarked that it is difficult to quote him briefly *and* fairly, which is to say, with a true sense of his finely nuanced style and ideas, I now have further reinforcement from his own remarks in the preface to *Portrait of Picasso as a Young Man*:

> ...there [is] real purpose to quoting other authors at greater length than is customary, and one is prepared to argue for the value of this as a practice. Style, after all, is revelation. Whether good or bad, style reveals the character of the writer who is perceiving the subject. To paraphrase another author is to deprive the reader, then, of the often unconscious but always instinctive critical judgement the reader is ready to make on the merits of the observer if given the opportunity to live a little while in the style (xii).

Few writers are considered as politically incorrect as Mailer today. This is unfortunate, unfair and paradoxical, considering that the cumulative weight of his works and his role as President of PEN (an international organization of writers), in which he led the battle for freedom of expression, have earned him the stature of senior statesman of American letters. In every arena of American life, he has left his enduring mark, and still he has not finished.

Why do I continue to follow Mailer's career so avidly? The answer lies in his constant commitment to personal and artistic growth. One could do worse than to adopt his example. He has temporarily postponed his work on part two of *Harlot's Ghost* and is instead working intensely on a book whose subject he has confided, apparently, to no one. Thus, although

I've had my say for the present, in a very real sense my study of Mailer will remain a work in progress throughout my life.

A further note to the reader may be in order. It is clear to all of us that literary criticism and our very language have changed. So have I. Thus, in this work I have become conscious of a growing personal subjectivity in my voice and in my choice of which books and themes to emphasize. In other words, I'm dealing with what engages me. That's what follows.

CHAPTER 1

MAILER AND MARILYN: PRISONERS OF SEX

Norman Mailer has been fascinated with the life and death of Marilyn Monroe for decades, although he has always said he never met her. According to Shelley Winters, he did meet her in 1948 in Hollywood at a rally for Henry Wallace, but Mailer doesn't remember this (Manso, 131-133). From his tangential references to her in *An American Dream,* to his two books about her, *Marilyn* and *Of Women and Their Elegance,* to his one-act play "Strawhead," he has treated her as a paradigmatic figure in the overheated world of the American sexual imagination. In a paradoxically complementary way, Mailer unwittingly found himself a similarly paradigmatic figure as the perceived antagonist of the Women's Movement in the late 1960s, a phenomenon he dealt with at some length in his 1971 book, *The Prisoner of Sex.* The issues, themes, and palpable tensions of heterosexual relationships illuminated there can ultimately be seen to inform much of his work and his own life. Even when dealing with the work of Henry Miller, in *Genius and Lust*, Mailer reveals his own artistic and personal predilections in these matters. Thus, a reading of these works reveals the coherence of Mailer's vision of Monroe, of women, and of heterosexual love.

Throughout his career of over half a century in literature and the public eye, Mailer has candidly aired his developing views on women and on heterosexuality. For almost as long, they have been misinterpreted, perversely or unwittingly: rewritten and obscured to suit the preconceptions and prejudices of his readers and critics. If this controversy reached a peak in the early seventies with the publication of *The Prisoner of Sex* (and the notable New York Town Hall symposium with Germaine Greer, Diana Trilling, and other prominent feminists), it began as early as *The Naked and the Dead*.

In this, his first published novel, Mailer touched repeatedly, if sometimes simplistically, on the attitudes of men towards women. These range from the predatory and irresponsible view of the syphilitic Private Woodrow Wilson of women as purely sexual objects who are "no fuggin' good," to the more sophisticated affectations of Lieutenant Robert Hearn, a liberal who doesn't like people (men *or* women) very much. As one of his sexual partners vitriolically accuses him:

> Hearn, she says, in her deep husky voice, you're a shell, you're nothing but a goddam shell. After you've had fifty thousand of us up here, you'll probably cut it off and hang it up to dry. You learned an acceptable wiggle somewhere along the line, and you think that's all you need to get by. You've got a faeces complex, haven't you, you can't stand being

touched. You get me so goddam mad, a million miles away aren't you, nothing ever hits
you. Nothing's worth touching (274).

The corrective to these cynical assessments is that of
Joey Goldstein, the nice Jewish boy from Brooklyn, an utterly
faithful husband. Gently reassuring the ambivalent Stanley, he
reveals his own kindness and decency:

Stanley deliberated a moment, seeking
a way to phrase it. "Do you ever get...well,
you know, jealous?" He spoke very softly so
that Brown could not hear them.

"Jealous? No I can't say I ever do,"
Goldstein said with finality. He had an inkling
of what was bothering Stanley, and automatically he tried to soothe him. "Listen," he said,
"I've never had the pleasure of meeting your
wife, but you don't have to worry about her.
These fellows that are always talking about
women that way, they don't know any better.
They've fooled around so much... " Goldstein
had a perception. "Listen, if you ever notice,
it's always the ones who go around with a lot
of, well, loose women who get so jealous. It's
because they don't trust themselves."

"Listen, you've got nothing to worry
about. Your wife loves you, doesn't she? Well
that's all you got to think about. A decent
woman who loves a man doesn't do anything
she shouldn't do" (421).

As early as 1955 in *The Deer Park*, Mailer was fascinated with, and adeptly portraying, the mercurial moods and ineffable psychology of the movie star in Lulu Meyers, a blonde actress with the "voice of a child," and the interpersonal transactions between an intellectual man and a sexually charged woman in the relationship of Charles Francis Eitel and Elena Esposito. Mailer would later write in *Marilyn*: "An old sultan with a thousand curses on his head is capable of smuggling anything into the mind and body of a young woman—less is known about the true transactions of fucking than any science on earth" (71). Nonetheless, Mailer has taken it upon himself to inherit the fallen mantle of Henry Miller and become the foremost professor of this sexual science.

In *An American Dream*, the "transactions of fucking" form the primary controlling metaphor of the novel. The infernal fornications of the Ruta passage introduce the essentially Manichaean vision which informs this novel and most of Mailer's subsequent work. The procreative love scene with Cherry that forms the novel's true center looks ahead to a vision of equality between lovers that would become central to the American consciousness later in the 1960s.

> Like diving on a cold winter day back to a warm pool, I was back in her, our wills now met, locked in a contest like an exchange of stares which goes on and on, wills which begin at last in the force of equality to water and to loose tears, to soften into some light which is shut away again by the will to force tears back, steel to steel, until steel shimmers in a mist of dew, is wiped, is wet again. I was pass-

ing through a grotto of curious lights, dark lights, like colored lanterns beneath the sea,…and a voice like a child's whisper on the breeze came up so faint I could hardly hear, "Do you want her?" it asked. "Do you really want her, do you want to know something about love at last?" and I desired something I had never known before, and answered; it was as if my voice had reached to its roots; and, "Yes," I said, "of course I do, I want love," but like an urbane old gentleman, a dry tart portion of my mind added, "Indeed, and what has one to lose?" and then the voice in a small terror, "Oh, you have more to lose than you have lost already, fail at love and you lose more than you can know." "And if I do not fail?" I asked back. "Do not ask," said the voice, "choose now!" and some continent of dread speared wide in me, rising like a dragon, as if I knew the choice were real, and in a lift of terror I opened my eyes and her face was beautiful beneath me in that rainy morning, her eyes were golden with light, and she said, "Ah, honey, sure," and I said sure to the voice in me, and felt love fly in like some great winged bird, some beating of wings at my back, and felt her will dissolve into tears, and some great deep sorrow like roses drowned in the salt of the sea came flooding from her womb and washed into me like a sweet honey of balm for all the bitter sores of my soul and for the first time in my life without passing through fire or straining the stones of my will, I came up from my body rather than down from my mind, I could not stop, some shield broke in me, bliss, and the honey she had given me I could only give back, all sweets to her womb....

"Son of a bitch," I said, "So that's what it's all about." And my mouth like a worn-out soldier fell on the heart of her breast (127-28).

But the novel also looks ahead to *Marilyn*, providing a glimpse of Mailer's lengthy fascination with her as an exemplar of the American sexual experience. He describes Cherry singing at a nightclub: "There was a champagne light which made her look like Grace Kelly, and a pale green which gave her a little of Monroe. She looked at different instants like a dozen lovely blondes..." (97). And at the novel's conclusion, when Rojack hallucinates one last telephone conversation with Cherry in heaven, she tells him, "Marilyn says to say hello" (269).

This brings us to *The Prisoner of Sex*. When Mailer learned that he was viewed as the archenemy of the women's liberation movement, he was, purportedly, surprised. As the story goes, Gloria Steinem revealed this distinction to him at lunch one day. When Mailer asked the reason, she said, "You might try reading your books someday" (19).

Mailer has always described himself as a counterpuncher, and this may be the most applicable metaphor for his responses to the women's movement. He begins by explaining the circumstances (notably the disintegration of his fourth marriage) which render the problems of heterosexual love more central than ever to his consciousness, then examines the central treatises of the movement. He discusses various factions, quoting at length from such documents as "The SCUM (Society for Cutting Up Men) Manifesto," "The NOW (National Organization for Women) Bill of Rights," and Germaine Greer's *The Female Eunuch*. But central to Mailer's discussion is Kate Millett's *Sexual Politics*, not least because a large portion of her work is devoted to an attack on his *American Dream*.

Mailer has written perceptive literary criticism before, but in the case of Millett his task is almost too easy. He shows her position to be virtually untenable, not only in regard to Mailer himself, but in her treatments of Henry Miller and D. H. Lawrence as well. By demonstrating the cavalier manner in which Ms. Millett quotes these authors out of context, Mailer calls into question the integrity of her methods as well as the rigidity of her doctrinaire line.

The technology of women's liberation is Mailer's next subject. An excerpt from an article by Ti-Grace Atkinson, dealing with extrauterine conception as a desirable goal, provides him an opening for digression upon one of his favorite subjects. For some years, Mailer has dealt in extramedical theories of his own (e.g., his often expressed belief that cancer can be caused by the repression of one's rage), which in turn bear upon his essentially Manichaean religious views. He likes to see things in terms of clear (if often complex) polarities, and the technology of conception lends itself much more readily to such treatment than did the Apollo 11 project, subject of *Of a Fire on the Moon*.

There's a striking difference in Mailer's stance between *Of a Fire on the Moon* and *The Prisoner of Sex*. In the former,

Mailer finds himself torn, puzzled. The polarity he has drawn in the past between sterile, satanic American technology and the fertile, God-oriented humanism he subscribes to, is blurred by Apollo 11. Repelled by the odorless, crew-cut world of NASA, Mailer is nonetheless awed by the massive achievement of the moon landing. Add to this the fact that Mailer has, for some years, appropriated the moon as one of his own favorite symbols, and the duality of his response assumes major proportions. Toward the end of *Of a Fire on the Moon*, Mailer, irritated by the drunken behavior of his good friend Eddie Bonetti in a restaurant, looks around at the vacuous, smug middle Americans at adjoining tables, and silently, dismally, thinks of his friend, "You've been drunk all summer…and *they* have taken the moon" (441).

The situation presented Mailer in *Of a Fire on the Moon* is not a happy one for him. He is forced to confront the possibility that the technology-oriented people of the establishment may, finally, have won the moon because in their dogged, unimaginative way they have earned the right to, while artists, intellectuals, and dropouts have submerged themselves in a lifestyle which has a sterility of its own.

No longer ambivalent, Mailer is unequivocal in *The Prisoner of Sex*: technology in sex and conception is, to him, utterly out of place. Sex must be funky, natural, unfettered. Puckishly, he proceeds to establish his credentials in treating contemporary scientific treatises. He recoils in mixed amusement and horror from the prospect of extrauterine conception and incubation, with their obvious *Brave New World* implications. He reacts with eloquent and poignant pain to the suggestions that machines are superior to men as sexual partners for women, and that every woman who ever claimed a vaginal orgasm was lying (All those wives, all those mistresses, lying?):

> What of his own poor experience? All lies?....
> If there were women who came as if lightning
> bolts had flung their bodies across the bed,
> were there not also women who came with
> the gentlest squeeze of the deepest walls of
> the vagina, women who came every way, even
> women who seemed never to come yet
> claimed they did, and never seemed to suffer?
> yes, and women who purred as they came and
> women who screamed, women who came as
> if a finger had been tickling them down a mile-
> long street and women who arrived with the
> firm frank avowal of a gentleman shaking
> hands, yes, if women came in every variety...even
> the most modest of men could know some-
> thing of that — then how to account for the
> declaration that vaginal orgasm was myth....
> Women, went the cry, liberate yourselves from
> the tyranny of the vagina. It is nothing but a
> flunky to the men (77-78).

But it is when he objects to experimentally demon-
strable scientific fact on purely emotional, even mystical,
grounds that Mailer is most compelling. After quoting at length
from various works on the feasibility of determining in advance the sex of one's child by artificially creating an alkaline
or acidic environment in the uterus, he reiterates strikingly
his fundamental belief that the quality of the act of conception
determines the quality of the offspring:

> One could make a boy or a girl if one was
> ready to swab vinegar or baking soda up one's
> love...if one believed a child begun in the
> juices of an unencumbered fuck was in no way
> superior to a baby made with an eye on the
> alkalinity factor...(214).

The difference between "unencumbered" conception
and technologically-monitored conception becomes for Mailer
a crucial one, for it is symptomatic of a larger political crisis:

> It was the measure of the liberal technologist
> and the Left totalitarian that they exhibited
> the social lust to make units of people... (129).

There's a totalitarian simplicity to the assumption that
all people are the same, a totalitarian method to the attempt to
"make units of people." Perhaps *Brave New World*, as it is made
to appear less outlandish by each new technological and social "advance," no longer frightens us.

What, finally, is Mailer saying in *The Prisoner of Sex*?
After the autobiographical background, the exercises in literary and scientific criticism, the elaborate digressions on suicide, homosexuality, cancer, what does he come out for? Ultimately, this book, egocentric as any he's ever written, is an
uncompromising, powerful, and often poignant statement of
Mailer's belief that if men and women are not to lose their
individual souls, the irrational magic in heterosexual love must
be carefully guarded. What many people seem to have forgot-
ten, and what Mailer helps us to remember, is that there are
differences between men and women, and that in these differ-

ences, in the tension, intensity, lust and love which depend upon them, lies much of the beauty of the human experience.

Toward the end of *The Prisoner of Sex*, Mailer, writing of D.H. Lawrence, says:

> Whoever believes that such a leap is not pos-
> sible across the gap, that a man cannot write
> of a woman's soul, or a white man of a black
> man, does not believe in literature itself (152).

He himself fleshes out this conceit in *Elegance*, a ficti-tious "autobiography" presented from the first person point of view of Marilyn Monroe, as though it were one of those "as told to" celebrity "autobiographies": Doris Day's story as told to A.E. Hotchner, or Marilyn's as told to Mailer. Apparently unable to leave his subject alone, Mailer subsequently wrote "Strawhead," a one-act play based on *Elegance* but conceived in an experimental mode strangely reminiscent of his 1967 off-Broadway dramatic adaptation of *The Deer Park*. "Strawhead" was staged for two weeks in 1986 at the Actors Studio Theater in New York to an appreciative audience of theatrical professionals. Ironically starring Mailer's daughter Kate, the play takes place entirely in Marilyn's mind, as she relives her memories in a virtually cinematic manner.

But the true story of the meshing of their minds was told in *Marilyn,* in which Mailer found in Monroe an Ameri-can symbol, a mass of paradoxes:

> She was the last of the myths to thrive in the
> long evening of the American dream…She was
> a cornucopia. She excited dreams of honey

for the horn. Yet she was more. She was a presence. She was ambiguous. She was the angel of sex, and the angel was in her detachment. For she was separated from what she offered. "None but Marilyn Monroe," wrote Diana Trilling, "could suggest such a purity of sexual delight. The boldness with which she could parade herself and yet never be gross, her sexual flamboyance and bravado which yet breathed an air of mystery and even reticence, her voice which carried such ripe overtones of erotic excitement and yet was the voice of a shy child—these complications were integral to her gift."...We heard her speak in that tiny tinkly voice so much like a dinnerbell, and it tolled when she was dead across that decade of the Sixties she had helped to create, across its promise, its excitement, its ghosts and its center of tragedy...[She was] a giant and an emotional pygmy; a lover of life and a cowardly hyena of death who drenched herself in chemical stupors; a sexual oven whose fire may rarely have been lit ... She was certainly more and less than the silver witch of us all. In her ambition, so Faustian,...her noble democratic longings intimately contradicted by the widening pool of her narcissism (where every friend and slave must bathe), we can see the magnified mirror of ourselves, our exaggerated and now all but defeated generation (16-17).

Does any of this sound familiar? In an interview with
Lenore Hershey in the *Ladies' Home Journal*, Mailer said:

> I've always wanted to enter a woman's mind.
> For some reason, though I never met her, I
> felt close to Marilyn Monroe. I feel the obvi-
> ous identity with her because she came out of
> nothing and achieved such notoriety. In a less
> embattled way, the same is true for me.

There are clearly similarities to be seen between Mailer
and Marilyn, despite their obvious differences in gender, intellectual achievement, family background, and above all, the
ability to survive the American celebrity experience. Both lived
the tarnished Horatio Alger myth. Mailer was able to criticize
it effectively, as in *An American Dream*, where the simplistic
myth of external success is rejected in favor of the existential
quest for self-definition; or in *Naked*, where Joey Goldstein's
blind acceptance of it is sad and faintly ridiculous. Marilyn
could never divorce herself wholly from it. And both were
indeed prisoners of sex, that essential element of the twentieth century American dream. For Marilyn, it was her stock in
trade, the trap she laid that became her own trap. For Norman,
it led to six marriages, nine children, and one of the primary
themes of more than thirty books.

Perhaps the most obvious way in which Mailer is
linked to Marilyn is in the supposition that she represents the
ultimate sexual fantasy for a man who has loved so many
women: the one he can never have, never meet. In response to
a question asked at the Miami Book Fair in November, 1988,
Mailer said of Monroe's marriage to Arthur Miller, "I always

thought I could have taken her from him because I would have understood her better. She needed understanding. But she hurt him badly; she probably would have killed me" (*Orlando Sun-Sentinel* 1E). On a more sophisticated and positive level, Mailer's *identification* with Monroe suggests, especially in *Elegance*, the announcement of a certain healthy androgyny by Mailer, a more successful one than that perceived by E.L. Doctorow in Hemingway's abortive attempt to remake himself in mid-life by the writing of *The Garden of Eden* (1986). (Doctorow suggests that Hemingway courageously recognized human androgyny and particularly his own, abandoning his strictly macho image, in this unfinished, posthumously published novel.) Thus, of Mailer's fanciful conjectures in *Marilyn* and *Elegance*, we may say what Ken Kesey's narrator Chief Bromden says at the outset of *One Flew over the Cuckoo's Nest*: "It's the truth even if it didn't happen."

Perhaps this sense of kinship is what most informs the poignancy of Mailer's farewell to Marilyn on behalf of us all:

> ... Let us hope her mighty soul and the mouse of her little one are both recovering their proportions in some fair and gracious home, and she will soon return to us from retirement. It is the devil of her humor and the curse of our land that she will come back speaking Chinese. Goodbye Norma Jean. Au revoir Marilyn. When you happen on Bobby and Jack, give the wink. And if there's a wish, pay your visit to Mr. Dickens. For he, like many another literary man, is bound to adore you, fatherless child (*Marilyn* 248).

Ultimately, the complex series of factors that have linked and continue to link Mailer and Marilyn has been persistently rendered simplistic by critics and admirers alike. These connections are at once improbable, ineffable, and paradoxically inevitable.

CHAPTER 2

THE POLITICAL WRITINGS: MAILER AS PSYCHIC OUTLAW

"The White Negro," Norman Mailer's seminal 1957 essay, casts a long shadow over the entire body of his work, as well as his life. A turning point in his political perceptions, it also provides the armature upon which *Advertisements for Myself* is built, defines the peculiarly American existentialism of *An American Dream*, and permeates the later work, perhaps most notably *The Executioner's Song*. Mailer's views on sex, violence and politics in American society are far from inchoate in his first three novels, *The Naked and the Dead*, *Barbary Shore* and *The Deer Park*; but the development of his personal and fictive philosophies shifts dramatically, looms into sharp focus with the advent of "The White Negro." Politically, it marks the fusion of Freud with Marx in his vision. Philosophically, it codifies the existential concepts which will be fleshed out in Stephen Rojack's quest for personal salvation in *An American Dream*. And personally, it foreshadows and clarifies his intense interest in the saga of Gary Gilmore as he gave it form in *The Executioner's Song*. The idea of the psychic outlaw as introduced in "The White Negro" has had a profound influence on the past four decades of Mailer's life and work, up to and including *Ancient Evenings*, *Tough Guys Don't Dance* and *Harlot's Ghost*.

I. Mailer's Political Writing

Throughout his fifty-odd years of writing, Mailer has been a consistently thorough critic of the American political scene. From his pointed judgments on incipient American fascism in such characters as General Cummings in *The Naked and the Dead*, to his vision of an Orwellian dystopia in *Barbary Shore* and his condemnation of the House Unamerican Activities Committee (HUAC) in *The Deer Park*, to his scathing denunciation of political and moral corruption in *An American Dream*, Mailer's fiction has been informed and conditioned by his astute political views. In his overtly political non-fiction writings, *The Presidential Papers*, *Cannibals and Christians*, *The Armies of the Night*, *Miami and the Siege of Chicago*, *St. George and the Godfather* and *Some Honorable Men*, he has intensely illuminated the flaws in American society and its political structure. Yet it is in "The White Negro" that Mailer's own radicalism and its development during the 1950s loom most sharply into focus. Here, the radical, the hipster, the American existentialist become one, as Mailer vitriolically and incisively lays bare the hypocrisies of America and prescribes the individual rebellion that he finds the only suitable response.

In "The White Negro," Mailer writes:

> The Second World War presented a mirror to
> the human condition which blinded anyone
> who looked into it...one was then obliged also
> to see that no matter how crippled and per-
> verted an image of man was the society he
> had created, it was nonetheless his creation,
> his collective creation...and if society was so
> murderous, then who could ignore the most
> hideous of questions about his own nature?
> (*Advertisements for Myself* 338).

Drawing its subject matter directly from that war, *The Naked and the Dead* proceeds to condemn both the perverted nature of society and the flawed human beings who create and perpetuate it.

In this novel, the American military hierarchy is presented as a microcosm of American society. The two primary antagonists in the virtually allegorical struggle between political ideologies posited by Mailer here are the liberal, Harvard-educated Lieutenant Hearn and the reactionary General Cummings. Robert Hearn defends humane values in the abstract, but doesn't like people, certainly not enlisted men, very much. Edward Cummings is a charismatic but coldly logical, highly effective and intelligent commander. He believes that Hitler was right in predicting a long period of ascendancy for the reactionaries, looks ahead to "When the war with Russia [will come]" (556) and persistently exacerbates the resentment and fear of the enlisted men by emphasizing class distinctions.

Hearn's futile attempts to rebel against Cummings or, more importantly, to align himself with the enlisted men, result in his personal defeat and a decidedly anticlimactic death through a sort of pincers movement from above and below him in the military (and hence the class) structure: Cummings acting through Major Dalleson as his rather dull tool, and Sergeant Croft acting through his somewhat passive accomplice, Julio Martinez. Mailer's implication is clear here: an essentially impotent American intellectual liberalism will be destroyed, not with a bang but a whimper, by a coalition of the power elite and the sullen but tacitly cooperative working class.

In *Barbary Shore*, Mailer's vision is perhaps more bleak. In retrospect, Mailer wrote of it in *Advertisements for Myself*:

> I was drawn...to write about an imaginary future...*Barbary Shore* was really a book to emerge from the bombarded cellars of my unconscious, an agonized eye of a novel which tried to find some amalgam of my new experience and the larger horror of that world which might be preparing to destroy itself. I was obviously trying for something which was at the very end of my reach, and then beyond it, and toward the end the novel collapsed into a chapter of political speech and never quite recovered. Yet, it could be that if my work is alive one hundred years from now, *Barbary Shore* will be considered the richest of my first three novels for it has in its high fevers a kind of insane insight into the psychic mysteries of Stalinists, secret policemen, narcissists, children, Lesbians, hysterics, revolutionaries—it has an air which for me is the air of our time, authority and nihilism stalking one another

> in the orgiastic hollow of this century... and
> yet much of my later writing cannot be un-
> derstood without a glimpse of the odd shadow
> and theme-maddened light *Barbary Shore* casts
> before it (94).

The novel is an ambitious failure. Set in a Brooklyn boarding house, it employs six highly allegorical characters to debate elaborate Marxist polemics and predict a totalitarian future. After a lengthy conflict between Leroy Hollingsworth, the government interrogator, and William McLeod, the former high-ranking Communist party official, Mailer's idealistic protagonist Mikey Lovett flees with little besides his existential will into a horrific world on the verge of class war. He tells his story under oppressive circumstances:

> Now, in the time I write, when other men
> besides myself must contrive a name, a story,
> and the papers they carry, I wonder if I do not
> possess an advantage. For I have been doing
> it longer, and am less tantalized by the memory
> of better years.
>
> Night comes and I am alone with a
> candle. What has been fanciful is now con-
> crete. Although the room in which I write has
> an electric circuit, it functions no longer. Time
> passes and I wait by the door, listening to the
> footsteps of roomers as they go out to work
> for the night. In fourteen hours they will be
> back (6-7).

And in a frightening, forceful conclusion, he predicts the conflict to come:

> Thus, time passes, and I work and I study, and I keep my eye on the door. Meanwhile, vast armies mount themselves, the world revolves, the traveller clutches his breast. From out of the unyielding contradictions of labor stolen from men, the march to the endless war forces its pace. Perhaps, as the millions will be lost, others will be created, and I shall discover brothers where I thought none existed (223).

Despite the fact that Mailer admittedly overextended himself in *Barbary Shore*, which is ultimately unsuccessful as either fiction or polemic, it represents an important step in his development toward a clearer statement of the relationship of the individual will to stifling societal strictures.

In *The Deer Park*, one of the basic dramatic conflicts lies in Charles Francis Eitel's refusal to testify cooperatively before the HUAC, the consequent foundering of his career as movie director, and his ultimate compromise and capitulation. In this, he lives up to his name: "I tell." But like Mikey Lovett under the tutelage of McLeod, Eitel's disciple Sergius O'Shaugnessy steadfastly resists such personal and political compromise, in the face of sexual and financial blandishments from Hollywood and bullying by government agents, and keeps the spirit of rebellion alive. Rejecting the simplistic American dream of materialism represented by the barren celluloid capital of falsity (the novel is set in a Hollywood suburb called Desert

D'Or: "desert of gold"), he goes to Mexico to become a writer, carrying with him Eitel's failed idealism:

> "So, do try, Sergius,' [Eitel] thought, 'try for that other world, the real world, where... nothing is more difficult to discover than a simple fact. And with the pride of the artist, you must blow against the walls of every power that exists, the small trumpet of your defiance.' (318).

The prepublication history of *The Deer Park* is extremely important to an understanding of Mailer's political and artistic development. After a shabby betrayal by his publisher, couched disingenuously in terms of the fear of censorship of a rather tame sexual passage (of which it is unnecessary to give a blow-by-blow account), Mailer came to some striking personal realizations:

> ... that my fine America which I had been at pains to criticize for so many years was in fact a real country which did real things and ugly things to the characters of more people than just the characters of my books (*Advertisements* 233).

In retrospect, Mailer sees the episode as a major milestone in his own development:

> And so as the language of sentiment would have it, something broke in me, but I do not

know if it was so much a loving heart, as a
cyst of the weak, the unreal, and the needy,
and I was finally open to my anger. I turned
within my psyche, I can almost believe, for I
felt something shift to murder in me. I finally
had the simple sense to understand that if I
wanted my work to travel further than others, the life of my talent depended on fighting
a little more, and looking for help a little less.
But I deny the sequence in putting it this way,
for it took me years to come to this fine point.
All I felt was that I was an outlaw, a psychic
outlaw, and I liked it, I liked it a good night
better than trying to be a gentleman...(234).

And the book of the psychic outlaw, the man set outside society, almost ten years in its gestation, was to take full-
blown form in *An American Dream*.

By 1965, when he published *An American Dream*,
Mailer was able to deal far more effectively with the postwar
political climate of America, on both literal and allegorical levels. Stephen Richards Rojack, war hero, former liberal congressman, professor of existential psychology, comes to represent what Mailer perceived as most idealistic and courageous
in the American national character, what became corrupted
by compromise with a venal society, and what may ultimately
be redeemed through courage, discipline and selfless, procreative love. Coming in mid-life to the edge of alcoholism, suicide, insanity and damnation, Rojack musters the existential
courage to love, and thus to find his way to personal salvation.

It is after making this personal commitment that Rojack is able to reject the power and wealth implicitly offered by his satanic father-in-law, Barney Oswald Kelly, and embrace a personal idealism which suggests hope for a similar redemption of the nation as well. This promise was to reach its full expression three years later in *The Armies of the Night*.

But the work which links these developing political expressions in Mailer's novels is the pivotal essay "The White Negro." Mailer himself writes in *Advertisements* of "... the radical bridge from Marx to Freud..." (365). As did earlier critics (notably J. Michael Lennon in 1977), Nigel Leigh suggests in his book, *Radical Fictions and the Novels of Norman Mailer* (1990), that between *Barbary Shore* and *An American Dream* the dramatic shift in Mailer's perception of the individual in relation to society was informed by his fictive fusion of Freud with Marx, a development marked by "The White Negro": "Only when Freud has been added to Marx does [Mailer] desire to 'create a revolution in the consciousness of our time' rather than a materialistic transformation in the means of production" (94). Leigh suggests that:

> Mailer's fundamental disagreement with radicalism in "The White Negro" and *An American Dream* lies in his reversal of the Marxist axiom that history precedes consciousness, that consciousness reflects historical process. What...Mailer (after 1957) argue[s] is that character structure can *create* social structure... in "The White Negro" and *An American Dream* the individual, once he achieves a radical/rootless condition, can presage social

change (94).

What, then, is Mailer's vision of society and the individual in "The White Negro"? If, as late as 1976, he could refer (in the preface to *Some Honorable Men*, a collection of his political writings) to his "bitterness at the conformity of the Eisenhower years" (vii), that bitterness was most overtly expressed here:

> One could hardly maintain the courage to be individual, to speak with one's own voice, for the years in which one could complacently accept oneself as part of an elite by being a radical were forever gone. A man knew that when he dissented, he gave a note upon his life which could be called in any year of overt crisis. No wonder then that these have been the years of conformity and depression. A stench of fear has come out of every pore of American life, and we suffer from a collective failure of nerve. The only courage, with rare exceptions, that we have been witness to, has been the isolated courage of isolated people (*Advertisements* 338-39).

And he refined his judgment with this effective distinction:

> A totalitarian society makes enormous demands on the courage of men, and a partially totalitarian society makes even greater de-

mands, for the general anxiety is greater. Indeed if one is to be a man, almost any kind of
unconventional action often takes dispropor-
tionate courage (338-39).

The only answer, to Mailer, is the existential rebellion
of the hipster:

> It is on this bleak scene that a phenomenon
> has appeared: the American existentialist—the
> hipster, the man who knows that if our col-
> lective condition is to live with instant death
> by atomic war, relatively quick death by the
> State...or with a slow death by conformity
> with every creative and rebellious instinct
> stifled,...why then the only life-giving answer
> is to accept the terms of death, to live with
> death as immediate danger, to divorce oneself
> from society, to exist without roots, to set out
> on that uncharted journey into the rebellious
> imperatives of the self (339).

Thus, Mailer's hipster/existentialist took as his model
the intuitive responses and rhythms of the black, his func-
tional paranoia, his sense of the immediate present. And in
this marriage of black instinct and white rebellion, "If marijuana was the wedding ring, the child was the language of
Hip... " (340).

The abstract concept of the white Negro is fleshed out
in strikingly effective fictional form in *An American Dream*, in
which Rojack intuitively commits himself to a fertile love for

Cherry and internalizes the strengths of the black singer Shago
Martin and, by implication, those of the American black. The
central scene of intimate confrontation between Rojack and
Shago is pointedly informed by the pervasive smell of marijuana and the use of hip argot. Insofar as these characters are
given allegorical value, Mailer seems to suggest here that what
is best in the American character can be redeemed with the
help of such downtrodden groups as poor women and blacks.

Towards the close of "The White Negro," Mailer attributes a potential idealism to the hipster/existentialist which
implies hope for the nation:

> it is…possible that many hipsters will come—
> if the crisis deepens—to a radical comprehen-
> sion of the horror of society…may yet come
> to an equally bitter comprehension of the slow
> relentless inhumanity of the conservative
> power which controls him from without and
> from within…indeed the hipster may come
> to see that his condition is no more than an
> exaggeration of the human condition, and if
> he would be free, then everyone must be free
> (355).

This is a position that seems to echo Sartre's doctrine of "good
faith."

At the conclusion of *An American Dream*, Rojack leaves
the country. But Mailer's inexorable movement towards hope
for America, and his intense love for her, is eloquently expressed three years later in *The Armies of the Night*. Here, in a
world of terrifying Manichaean choices, the individual will,

expressed by the large-scale idealism of thousands of anti-war protesters, *may* finally portend redemption for the nation itself:

> Brood on that country who expresses our will. She is America, once a beauty of magnificence unparalleled, now a beauty with a leprous skin. She is heavy with child—no one knows if legitimate—and languishes in a dungeon whose walls are never seen. Now the first contractions of her fearsome labor begin—it will go on: no doctor exists to tell the hour. It is only known that false labor is not likely on her now, no, she will probably give birth, and to what?—the most fearsome totalitarianism the world has ever known? or can she, poor giant, tormented lovely girl, deliver a babe of a new world brave and tender, artful and wild? Rush to the locks. God writhes in his bonds. Rush to the locks. Deliver us from our curse. For we must end on the road to that mystery where courage, death, and the dream of love give promise of sleep (288).

II. Mailer as Psychic Outlaw

Mailer's persistent distinction between the institutional violence of the State as opposed to the spontaneous violence of the individual, and his insistently pejorative judgment of the former, is most unattractively illuminated by the notorious statement in "The White Negro" where Mailer justifies the actions of two hypothetical eighteen-year-old hoodlums murdering a weak candy-store owner (*Advertisements* 347). But this salient passage qualifies his example:

> The strength of the psychopath is that he knows (where most of us can only guess) what is good for him and what is bad for him at exactly those instants when an old crippling habit has become so attacked by experience that the potentiality exists to change it, to replace a negative and empty fear with an outward action, even if...the action is to murder. [He] murders—if he has the courage—out of the necessity to purge his violence, for if he cannot empty his hatred then he cannot love, his being is frozen with implacable self-hatred for his cowardice (347).

This is expressed fictionally in *An American Dream*, in which Stephen Rojack's murder of his estranged wife sets him on an existential journey into the labyrinthine recesses of his inner self, while the State pursues him with its cumbersome legal machinery; but Rojack's real struggle is not with monolithic bureaucracy. Rather, it is his battle to redeem himself by finding love, religious salvation, and above all existential self-determination in a world that fairly reeks of palpable evil.

This concept profoundly informs Mailer's life as well as his work. Mailer's biographers have dealt at length with the motives and circumstances of his November 20, 1960 stabbing of his second wife Adele Morales (Mills 223; Rollyson 137). Although there are apparent parallels to this incident in *Deaths for the Ladies (and other disasters)*, notably: "So long as

you use a knife,/there's some love left" (n.p.), one must accept
Mailer's statement in his *Playboy* interview that there is no direct link (Lucid 290-91).

Violence has pervaded Mailer's work, both fiction and
non-fiction, from *The Naked and the Dead* to *Harlot's Ghost*.
But it is never gratuitous violence. In a 1987 interview, I spoke
to him about the negative responses many critics have had to
the violence and sex in his work. I mentioned the following
passage from his 1978 introduction to *A Transit to Narcissus* (a
novel he wrote before *The Naked and the Dead*, which remained
unpublished for over thirty years) in which he wrote:

> I do not recognize the young man who wrote
> this book, I do not even like him very much,
> and yet I know that he must be me because
> his themes are mine, his ambition is as large
> for his age as my ambition would ever become,
> and I am not even without an odd regard for
> him. If I understand what he is trying to say,
> then he is close to saying the unsayable. The
> most terrible themes of my own life: the near-
> ness of violence to creation, and the whiff of
> murder just beyond every embrace of love are
> his themes also (x).

I asked him whether he felt these thematic preoccupations had hurt him in terms of critical responses to his work:

> It occurs to me that although you're obviously
> evolving over these forty-odd years into a dif-
> ferent kind of writer all the time, these the-

matic preoccupations really have remained constant—not static but constant—and I wonder if you feel that being thus preoccupied has hurt you, in that so many critics have been shortsighted about roundly attacking your work for those reasons (Leeds 2).

His response was:

At the least it's made me hard to read for a number of people. They approach my books with anxiety, precisely the anxiety that street people feel when they're walking down the street and expect trouble. Most people who read books are...at least superficially, gentle and reflective and civilized. They read books to avoid the street. While books about violence are exotic to such readers, they are also disturbing. And I think [my books] are doubly disturbing because what I am saying is: Look, I'm not asking you to read about violence so you can have a good read, I'm saying there's a whole lot of meaning in violence. That it's one aspect of a world-wide violence which appropriates us. You know I've been saying from the beginning, of course, there's individual violence versus the violence of the State. It takes a thousand forms (2).

In *The Executioner's Song*, Gary Gilmore's senseless, brutal, but spontaneous murders are held in opposition to

the State's legal execution of Gilmore. Mailer has said of
Gary Gilmore:

> I found him a funny man and parts of him I
> understand perfectly; other parts of him to this
> day I don't have a clue. He had a quirky dull
> streak that I've never gotten near, but the side
> of him that wanted to die I understand per-
> fectly. It was almost like he was dramatizing
> one of my favorite notions, that the soul can
> die before the body, and was quite aware of
> that and was determined not to let that hap-
> pen and in that sense was heroic (Leeds 10).

The Gilmore case spilled over into Mailer's own life
when, during the writing of *The Executioner's Song*, Mailer received a letter from Jack Henry Abbott, a federal prisoner with
whom Mailer began a lengthy correspondence. The ensuing
events are public knowledge. Mailer (and several others in the
literary world) helped Abbott gain parole, helped him publish
an edited version of his letters from prison under the title *In
the Belly of the Beast* (1981), and wrote an introduction for that
volume. Virtually on the day of publication, Abbott killed again,
just as the *New York Times Book Review* hit the streets with
Terence Des Pres' rhapsodic front-page review:

> We have before us the most intense, I might
> even say the most fiercely visionary book of
> its kind in the American repertoire of prison
> literature. *In the Belly of the Beast* is awesome,
> brilliant, perversely ingenious; its impact is

indelible, and as an articulation of penal night-
mare it is completely compelling (Des Pres 1).

In 1983 came *Ancient Evenings*, the "big book" Mailer
had been promising to write throughout his career, more than
ten years in the making. This massive book, as large as its
author's ambitions, has been both praised and reviled. A thor-
oughly researched testimony to Mailer's disciplined scholarship, it is nonetheless a work of pure imagination. Recogniz-
ably the product of Mailer's life-long thematic preoccupations,
it is different from anything he has previously written. Some
of the scenes he evokes burn indelible visual images into the
reader's mind, notably his description of the Battle of Kadesh
(1294 B.C.), which has as much to say to us of war today as
The Naked and the Dead did in 1948; or its aftermath, during
which Menenhetet walks about the battlefield, lighted by a
thousand fires and emblazoned with ten thousand brutalities,
accompanied by Hera-Ra, a lion of ferocious and playful moods.
Set in Egypt of the nineteenth and twentieth dynas-
ties (1290-1100 B.C.), the novel opens in the tomb of a dead
man, Menenhetet II, and from the outset the writing is both
lyrical and terrifying:

> But now the mills of vituperation were turn-
> ing again. Like a serpent whose insides have
> blown apart, I gave up, sued for peace, and
> gave birth to my bloody clotting history of
> coiled and twisted eviscerate. Some totality of
> me went out of my belly...I would be no
> longer what I had been. My soul felt pained,
> humbled, furious at loss, and still arrogant as

beauty itself. For the pain had ceased and I
was new. I had a body again (4-5).

At the end of the novel, Menenhetet II unites with his
great-grandfather, Menenhetet I, for the painful and courage-
wracking journey through the Land of the Dead to a new in-
carnation that looks forward hopefully to our own future. But
in between lies the body of the work, related by Menenhetet I,
a compelling figure who tells the story of his four lives, spanning 180 years, during which he rose from peasant to chari-
oteer to general; became a harem master, magician, grave-rob-
bing priest, brothel-keeper; endured betrayal and violent death;
enjoyed great wealth, the intimate friendship of Pharaohs and
the sexual favors of queens.

Anyone familiar with Mailer's work can easily tell that
only he could have written this book. Behind Menenhetet I/
II stand Cummings, Croft, Rojack, Sergius O'Shaugnessy, D.J.,
Henry Miller, and the ghost of Gary Gilmore. This book car-
ries their lessons and Mailer's themes a long step further. Here
are the preoccupation with reincarnation and the rich possi-
bilities of human sexuality; but above all, the vision of this
book is informed by violence, from the Battle of Kadesh to
the solitary pub-crawl of Bone-Smasher, perhaps an early
white Negro.

Mailer has, characteristically, taken enormous risks
here. He shows great nerve in expecting his readers to accept
this world he posits; yet, in his farthest flights of imagination,
he succeeds ultimately in evoking a willing suspension of disbelief. *Ancient Evenings*, long but never tedious, unremittently
violent, is a demanding experience that well repays the reader's
participation. It is powerful, pungent, visceral stuff, not for

everyone. But those willing to take this epic journey through blood, fire and excrement will be lifted by Mailer's soaring conclusion. Just as fruition grows out of dung, the hope of an existential new beginning grows out of the vices and brutality—the ultimate courage—of man.

Tough Guys Don't Dance, as I note elsewhere, leads us back to *An American Dream.* As the basis for Mailer's movie of the same title starring Ryan O'Neal and Isabella Rossellini, it piques our interest. But this is territory he had mined for better paydirt twenty years earlier in *An American Dream,* the work most crucial to Mailer's vision of the importance of violence in the existential definition and creation of the self. In this novel, he deals in a memorable passage with the cosmic order posited by his later works, and the disruption of that order, the tear in its fabric caused by murder:

> No, men were afraid of murder, but not from
> a terror of justice so much as the knowledge
> that a killer attracted the attention of the gods;
> then your mind was not your own, your anxi-
> ety ceased to be neurotic, your dread was real.
> Omens were as tangible as bread. There was
> an architecture to eternity which housed us
> as we dreamed, and when there was murder,
> a cry went through the market places of sleep.
> Eternity had been deprived of a room. Some-
> where the divine rage met a fury (192).

Again, I asked Mailer: "This sense of the cosmic order and an embattled God is something that obviously has pervaded your work, but do you feel that in recent years it's been expanded, refined, changed in any way?"

His response:

> I think it has. You know, if I end up writing a
> few more good books then those refinements
> ideally will find their way into that. I still
> would subscribe to every single thing that's
> said there. That hasn't changed a bit...But I
> find that idea you've just quoted is the key to
> all my ideas. There are little variations on it
> all the time, but...it hasn't really changed that
> much. I'm still trying to find a way to em-
> body all that in a book where it truly works
> for a reader who's never encountered these
> notions before (Leeds 10).

Just as Mailer was not content, as the censorship laws
began to fall in the early 1960s, to treat human sexual activity
as merely another valid form of human expression, but instead made the sexually graphic Rojack/Ruta scene the basis
for the controlling metaphor of his Manichaean vision in *An
American Dream*, he daringly does the same with violence.
Rojack's murder of Deborah, whether viewed literally or alle-
gorically, cuts him loose from the girdling structures of external identity that have held him up, and sets him on the path of
the outlaw. We can see, in retrospect, that Mailer has been
preparing us for this as early as *Deaths for the Ladies,* in which
he provides us thematic previews of *An American Dream*. Further, in a new introduction *to Deaths* written years later, concluding with his response to a vicious review it received in
Time magazine, he gives us a key to the visceral insemination

and gestation of *Dream*:

> Now, on the comfortable flank of this remi-
> niscence, I think I may have been fortunate
> to get so paltry a reception on *Deaths for the
> Ladies*. For if I had been treated well, I might
> have kept floating in a still little pond, and
> drowned my sorrow for myself in endless wine
> and scraps of paper and folios of further po-
> ems. Instead, the review in *Time* put iron into
> my heart again, and rage, and the feeling that
> the enemy was more alive than ever, and
> dirtier in the alley, and so one had to mend,
> and put on the armor, and go to war, go out
> to war again, and try to hew huge strokes with
> the only broadsword God ever gave you, a
> glimpse of something like Almighty prose
> (n.p.).

In this, Mailer has succeeded: He has both written and *lived* the life of the white Negro, the psychic outlaw.

CHAPTER 3

BOXING AS A MORAL PARADIGM IN MAILER'S WORK

Boxing has provided a significant moral paradigm throughout much of Mailer's life and work. In his seminal essay entitled "Death" in *The Presidential Papers*, Mailer uses the first Sonny Liston/Floyd Patterson championship bout as a point of departure from which to develop a profound series of perceptions about the American national temperament, particularly that of blacks. In *King of the Hill* and more strikingly in *The Fight* he deals nominally with a specific championship bout, but goes beyond journalism to find certain normative precepts in the sport. But there is another level on which boxing informs and conditions Mailer's vision: in his fiction, most notably *An American Dream* and *Tough Guys Don't Dance*, boxing experiences help define the protagonists. Stephen Richards Rojack and Tim Madden respectively find "the reward of the ring" (*Dream* 16) applicable to their existential quests for self. Ultimately, Mailer's views on boxing are far from simplistic.

From the powerful account of Benny Paret's death in the ring at the hands of Emile Griffith to his statements to me about the ill-fated conclusion to Muhammad Ali's career to his 1988 article on Mike Tyson, "Fury, Fear, Philosophy," Mailer has found in this arena of ritualized violence a rich source of perception about the human condition. In fact, in his 1993 essay in *Esquire*, "The Best Move Lies Next to the Worst" (reprinted in *The Time of Our Time*), he deals with his own boxing experiences at the Gramercy Gym with José Torres, Ryan O'Neal and others. The title of the piece comes from the comparison of boxing to chess (*Time*, 1045-1052).

I believe it's best to confront the central issue here at the outset. Mailer has, indeed, perceived gladiatorial confrontation and violence as a central metaphor for his own artistic and personal struggles for growth, fulfillment, salvation. As he muses retrospectively upon a turning point in his career during his personal crises of the early 1960s,

> ... the review in *Time* [of *Deaths for the Ladies*] put iron into my heart again, and rage, and the feeling that the enemy was more alive than ever, and dirtier in the alley, and so one had to mend, and put on the armor, and go to war, go out to war again, and try to hew huge strokes with the only broadsword God ever gave you, a glimpse of something like almighty prose (*Existential Errands* 204).

Very well, then: Mailer unabashedly uses violent confrontation as a touchstone for his vision of life and art. He has persistently perceived himself as embattled. But witness the artistic regeneration, the prolific and truly significant output that has resulted as a direct consequence of this attitude.

Mailer's significant writing about boxing begins with *The Presidential Papers* in the long and riveting essay entitled "Death," originally titled "Ten Thousand Words a Minute," one of his "Big Bite" columns for *Esquire*. Not only does this piece prefigure and announce the new mode of Mailer's non-fiction writing in the late 1960s and 1970s, notably *The Armies of the Night*, it is the key to his fascination with boxing.

The first Patterson/Liston fight provides Mailer an opportunity to embark on a series of sophisticated statements on boxing and the national disposition. But the center of the piece, as the title suggests, is the brutal killing of Benny Paret in the ring by Emile Griffith. Let us deal with the most hideous aspects of boxing first. Unlike most bouts, this one was fueled by an intense hatred between the fighters. Here is Mailer's description of the climax:

> In the twelfth, Griffith caught him. Paret got trapped in a corner. Trying to duck away, his left arm and his head became tangled on the wrong side of the top rope. Griffith was in like a cat ready to rip the life out of a huge boxed rat. He hit him eighteen right hands in a row, an act which took perhaps three or four seconds, Griffith making a pent-up whimpering sound all the while he attacked, the right hand whipping like a piston rod which has broken through the crankcase, or like a baseball bat demolishing a pumpkin.... I had never seen

one man hit another so hard and so many times. Over the referee's face came a look of woe as if some spasm had passed its way through him, and then he leaped on Griffith to pull him away. It was the act of a brave man. Griffith was uncontrollable. His trainer leaped into the ring, his manager, his cut man, there were four people holding Griffith, but he was off on an orgy, he had left the Garden, he was back on a hoodlum's street. If he had been able to break loose from his handlers and the referee, he would have jumped Paret to the floor and whaled on him there.

And Paret? Paret died on his feet. As he took those eighteen punches something happened to everyone who was in psychic range of the event. Some part of his death reached out to us. One felt it hover in the air. He was still standing in the ropes, trapped as he had been before, he gave some little half-smile of regret, as if he were saying, 'I didn't know I was going to die just yet,' and then, his head leaning back but still erect, his death came to breathe about him ("Death" 244-45).

This event was not, of course, taken lightly by the public:

There was shock in the land.... There were editorials, gloomy forecasts that the Game was dead. The managers and the prizefighters got

together. Gently, in thick, depressed hypocrisies, they tried to defend their sport (245).

Mailer goes on to delve into that species of blood religion to which fight people adhere and the kind of mystery it
has lent to the works of such writers as D.H. Lawrence and
Ernest Hemingway. And what of Mailer's own response?

Something in boxing was spoiled.... I loved
it with freedom no longer. It was more like
somebody in your family was fighting now.
And the feeling one had for a big fight was no
longer clear of terror in its excitement. There
was awe in the suspense (247-48).

Professional boxing, then, presents difficult moral
problems to Mailer as well as to any humane person. This
does not, I submit, obviate its significance in Mailer's work as
a test of courage. I would suggest that it is in the exercise of
disciplined skill, resourcefulness, stoicism, the force of will in
the face of risk, that the human spirit is capable of reaching its
peak expression.

Another case in point is *King of the Hill*, a modest little
book originally published as a long article in *Life* magazine (with
photographs by Frank Sinatra), dealing with Muhammad Ali's
hard-fought defeat at the hands of Joe Frazier after his three
year enforced layoff from boxing. As in "Death," the opponents
assume symbolic, almost mythic proportions. Central to this is
Mailer's pervasive Manichaean vision of the cosmos, even down
to Ali's twin poodles named "Angel" and "Demon." But the conclusion is most significant to Mailer's later work:

... yet Ali got up, Ali came sliding through the last two minutes and thirty-five seconds of this heathen holocaust in some last exercise of the will, some iron fundament of the ego not to be knocked out, and it was then as if the spirit of Harlem finally spoke and came to rescue and the ghosts of the dead in Vietnam, something held him up before arm-weary triumphant near-crazy Frazier who had just hit him the hardest punch ever thrown in his life and they went down to the last few seconds of a great fight, Ali still standing and Frazier had won.

The world was talking instantly of a rematch. For Ali had shown America what we all had hoped was secretly true. He was a man. He could bear moral and physical torture and he could stand. And if he could beat Frazier in the rematch we would have at last a national hero who was hero of the world as well... (*King* 92-93).

Ali *was* a national hero, for his moral and physical courage. His heroism had fascinated Mailer for years. In a short piece, "An Appreciation of Cassius Clay," he wrote: "[I] don't want to get started writing about Muhammad Ali, because I could go on for a book" (*Errands* 264). He went on to condemn Ali's exclusion from boxing because of his conscientious objection to the Vietnam War and concluded: "Therefore we are all deprived of an intimate spectacle which was taking place in public—the forging of a professional artist of extraordinary dimensions...he was bringing a revolution to the theory of boxing... " (264). And when I asked him, "... now that it's pretty well documented that Ali has been damaged by boxing, do you love the sport as much as you did?" Mailer responded, "Well, I don't think I love it as much as I used to. One reason is because he's out of it" (Leeds 1).

All of this of course points directly to Mailer's most significant work on boxing, *The Fight*. Suffice it to say that Mailer's obsessive preoccupation with existentialism and Manichaean polarities, his newly found fascination with African mysticism and the concept of *N'golo* (or force), his vision of Muhammad Ali as artist and hero, find their serendipitous confluence here.

As in virtually all of his work after 1968, Mailer treats a factual situation, and the people involved, in terms of highly subjective and fascinating digressions. Thus, in addition to an in-depth account of the fight and the circumstances preceding and following it, the reader is offered observations on African religion and politics, allusions to Hemingway, Hunter Thompson and George Plimpton, and further candid insights into Mailer himself: the status of his projected big novel, his compulsion to walk parapets, his hatred of jogging. Most amusing, however, is the self-deprecating anecdote in which Mailer, returning late at night along a jungle path on which he had been doing road work with Ali, hears a lion roar. He proceeds through a series of serio-comic reactions, culminating in the fantasy that he is about to be eaten by "Hemingway's own lion" waiting all these years for a fit substitute, and the final recognition that the lion he hears is probably caged in the city's zoo (91-92). This announces, I believe, an attractive new modesty in Mailer.

Round 2:
Violence in Personal Confrontation Outside the Ring

What I consider more significant here is Mailer's fictive vision of fighting. Violence in personal confrontations outside the ring, both in heterosexual relationships and between male adversaries, is central to Mailer's fiction. Christian Messenger, in a related article, makes some interesting points, but I think it's a critical commonplace to trot out Mailer's 1959 story, "The Time of Her Time," as the beginning of all this. As early as *A Transit to Narcissus*, Mailer was already concerned with the smoldering violence between sexual partners, alluding to "the most terrible themes of my own life: the nearness of violence to creation, and the whiff of murder just beyond every embrace of love... " (Introduction x).

And the darkest side of this vision is disturbingly revealed in *The Armies of the Night*, when Mailer writes with horror of Federal Marshals and American soldiers brutally beating young women during the night after the 1967 march on the Pentagon: Such men, he suggests, "may never have another opportunity like this—to beat a woman without having to make love to her" (276).

It's true that in "The Time of Her Time," Sergius O'Shaugnessy, just back from Mexico after the end of *The Deer Park*, does throw Denise Gondelman "a fuck the equivalent of a fifteen round fight" ("Time" in *Advertisements* 501). Sergius has been a boxer in the Air Force, and in bed he and Denise are "like two club fighters" (490). But it is she who gets in the last literal punch: "I might have known she would have a natural punch. My jaw felt it for half an hour after she was gone..." (454). And in the story's last line, he muses that "... like a real killer, she did not look back, and was out the door before I could rise to tell her that she was a hero fit for me" (503). This is, therefore, a battle of equals, which prefigures embryonically the growth toward the graceful, loving equality of the central Rojack/Cherry passage in *An American Dream*.

The extended fighting metaphor reaches its peak in *An American Dream*. Stephen Rojack is an amateur boxer, and clearly the central bout of the novel is the vitriolic and deadly scene in the opening chapter when, in a surprisingly even match, he fights and kills his powerful, witch-like wife, Deborah. But I must point out yet again that Rojack does not, as Kate Millett suggests, "get away with murder" (*Sexual Politics* 15). Instead, this scene, with its pervasive parallel imagery of combat and sex is part of a cohesive and symmetrical pattern of symbolism which unifies the novel tonally, structurally and thematically. After a series of mutual insults and the escalating fury of an intense physical struggle, Rojack strangles Deborah:

> ... spasms began to open in me, and my mind cried out then, "Hold back! you're going too far, hold back!" I could feel a series of orders whiplike tracers of light from my head to my arm, I was ready to obey. I was trying to stop, but pulse packed behind pulse in a pressure up to thunderhead; some blackbiled lust, some desire to go ahead not unlike the instant one comes in a woman against her cry that she is without protection came bursting with rage from out of me...(35-36).

This inflammatory scene introduces a more significant bout: that of Rojack with himself, in the heroic struggle to purge his own moral weakness and set out on that terrifying journey into the labyrinthine recesses of the self, on the existential quest for the true identity that lies at his core. This quest is punctuated by successively more frightening confrontations: first the scene of hellish fornication with the "Nazi" maid, Ruta, which establishes the allegorical nature of Rojack's pilgrimage to salvation in an infernal world of Manichaean choices; then with Ike "Romeo" Romalozzo, a brutal and corrupt ex-boxer; and with police Lieutenant Roberts, who is described after Rojack outwits him as a crooked wrestler who hadn't known it was his night to lose.

Penultimately, he faces Shago Martin, who in a scene of intimate violence redolent of sexual connection ("I got a whiff of his odor…a smell of full nearness, as if we'd been in bed for an hour " [*Dream* 182]) teaches Rojack something about nobility and forgiveness and passes on to him the phallic power (as epitomized in Shago's totemic umbrella) necessary for his climactic confrontation with Barney Oswald Kelly.

Insofar as each of these characters has allegorical as well as literal value in the novel, Rojack's struggles with them may be seen as confrontations with the worst aspects of himself, which he must overcome and purge. On a larger scale, his progress is a peculiarly American one, a repudiation of the false American dream of meretricious corruption and an embracing of a new, true American dream of authenticity of self. Rojack comes to represent what was best in the American character after World War II, what was shamelessly corrupted, and what Mailer suggests may be redeemed by courage, discipline and a commitment to selfless heterosexual love. And he does this with the aid of representatives of marginalized groups: Shago and Cherry.

Tough Guys Don't Dance is a lesser novel: a pale reflection, a distant echo of the masterful American Dream. But a few points are worth touching on. Again, Tim Madden has been an amateur boxer in his youth. He does fight and defeat Spider Nissen and Stoodie, the badness twins, with the aid of "Stunts," his dog, who dies with Spider's knife in his heart. But despite initial, ambiguous appearances, Tim does not hurt, does not kill women, or kill anyone for that matter. But Patty Lareine, his wife, does kill Jessica Pond. In fact, two women are murderers: Madeleine Falco also shoots her husband, the corrupt Chief of Police Alvin Regency. Significantly, Tim Madden refuses the tempting suggestion of Patty Lareine that he kill her then husband, Meeks Wardley Hilby III, and by the novel's end is capable of compassionate tenderness towards the suicidal, homosexual Wardley. Further, Tim establishes an almost friendly relationship with Patty's hostile, dangerous black lover, Bolo Green (a.k.a. "Mr. Black"). Most important, like Rojack at the conclusion of An American Dream, Tim is shown to fight his true battle with himself and his own fears and weaknesses.

Thus, in this novel, as in virtually all of Mailer's work, combat with adversaries is most pivotal as an external manifestation of the true central struggle within oneself against the ignoble, ignominious emotions of cowardice and moral sloth. Courage, personal discipline, stoicism, the leap of faith essential to love, the definition and celebration of the existential self: these values are not outmoded. They never will be.

Round 3

Scorsese vs. Mailer: Boxing as Redemption In *Raging Bull* and *An American Dream*

 Raging Bull (1980), Martin Scorsese's penetrating treatment of Jake LaMotta's boxing career and the role of violence as it defined LaMotta both in and out of the ring, provides a number of parallels (and some significant differences in focus) to Mailer's vision of boxing.

 Unlike Mailer, who has been fascinated by boxing from the outset, Scorsese came reluctantly to the sport as an artistic subject. When Robert DeNiro gave him the book *Raging Bull* and suggested it as a film project, Scorsese recalls his response was: "A boxer? I don't like boxing.... The idea...was something I didn't—couldn't—grasp" (Kelly 122).

 By contrast, Mailer has consistently treated violent confrontation as a central metaphor for his own artistic and personal struggles for growth, fulfillment, salvation. When younger, especially in middle age, he was known for his refusal to avoid a brawl. This ethic has been evident for at least forty years in his writing.

 An interesting confluence of life and art informs the comparison between Scorsese and Mailer. In his seminal novel *An American Dream*, Mailer introduces a brief but significant confrontation between his protagonist, Stephen Richards Rojack (a university professor, television personality and amateur boxer) and a brash retired prizefighter, Ike "Romeo" Romalozzo. This provides a crucial test of courage for Rojack in the series of challenges by which he wins the love of Cherry Melanie and finds his way to personal salvation and an existential definition of self. Romeo seems to be modeled on Jake LaMotta.

Despite the pitfalls of biographical criticism, it's difficult to ignore the similarities between Romalozzo and LaMotta or the fact that Mailer drew upon personal experience in this scene. Each of Mailer's biographers to date (Mills 271, Manso 374, Rollyson 155) recounts the story of how Mailer first met Beverly Bentley, who was to become his fourth wife and the prototype for Cherry in *An American Dream*. Mailer and his friend Roger Donoghue, a world middleweight contender from 1946-1952 with whom Mailer frequently sparred, and who says "Tough writers *can* fight" (Manso 677), were drinking at P.J. Clarke's on the East Side of Manhattan one spring night in 1963 when "a pretty blond actress, Beverly Bentley, walked in, accompanied by former middleweight boxing champion Jake LaMotta" (Mills 271). Donoghue, who knew Bentley, introduced her to Mailer. According to Donoghue,

> I don't know what happened to LaMotta that night, but a couple of years ago, in fact, I ran into Norman and asked how the divorce from Beverly was going. He says, '... It's goin' tough.' Then we got talking about the movie *Raging Bull*—it had just been released—and he cracked, 'Maybe I shoulda married Jake LaMotta' (Manso 374).

Mailer, like his character Stephen Rojack, took the boxer's date home: according to Beverly, "... I was attracted to the vulnerability beneath his tough act. He walked me to my apartment. That night he was wonderful in bed" (Mills 271). The intervening events, in life unrecorded by any witness, are quite dramatic in the fictional scene in *An American Dream*.

Romeo, who "had a very bad reputation in the ring" (*Dream* 93) tells Cherry, "They're going to make a movie of my life" (101). The projected movie is described by Romeo in terms of clichés: "Story of a kid who goes bad, turns straight, goes bad again…. It's the fault of the company he keeps. Bad influences. Cheap whiskey. Broads" (101). He concludes, "If they get a good enough actor to play my part they are going to make a very good movie" (101).

No better actor could have played LaMotta than Robert DeNiro in his Academy Award-winning performance in *Raging Bull*, and the film itself rises far above the Hollywood stereotypes described by Romeo. Yet the peculiarly American quality of the story as told in bald outline echoes the deceptively simple surface of Rojack's tale, that of a man who murders his wife, meets a beautiful blonde and survives the American experience intact. Thus, both Scorsese and Mailer are able to take hackneyed situations and transmute them into true art that transcends the trite and predictable.

In the novel, the Romeo passage becomes one of the dramatic turning points of Rojack's quest for personal salvation through courage. Although no blow is struck, Rojack's refusal to retreat before Romeo's crude bullying helps him grow morally and win the opportunity to begin his redemptive relationship with Cherry. More significantly, this scene raises the central issue of the similarities and differences between Mailer's vision of boxing and personal confrontation in such protagonists as Rojack, and that of Scorsese and DeNiro in their portrayal of LaMotta.

Both Rojack and LaMotta seek their identities largely through courage and violence; and each achieves a form of spiritual purification only after tempering, even renouncing, this violence. As Mary Pat Kelly writes in *Martin Scorsese: A Journey*,

> Scorsese and DeNiro...have taken apart this man, Jake LaMotta, and reconstructed not the fighter of reality, but the figure of a man so unconscious of his own feelings and emotions that he can speak only through violence.... Yet Jake is conscious of the "bad things" he has done, and sees his defeats as a kind of punishment. His rise to the championship and his relationships with...women...seem marked with a gratuitous brutality—for example, he destroys the face of the good-looking fighter whom his wife Vicki [sic] has admired (121).

Kelly goes on to suggest that at the film's end, Jake, shouting "I am not an animal!" in his jail cell and in a subsequent scene embracing his brother Joey (Joe Pesci), "faces himself and somehow, redemption begins.... A man recognizes his own soul" (121).

Stephen Rojack is a far more cerebral and introspective character, but his rebirth, too, comes from purging his rage and ultimately achieving a more profound knowledge of himself.

A crucial point of departure between Scorsese's vision of regeneration and Mailer's lies in their respective treatments of their protagonists' relationships with women. Rojack sets out on his pilgrimage to salvation by murdering his estranged wife Deborah with his bare hands, a scene rendered in pointedly combative terms. Deborah is described as a "prep-school bully," a "wrestler," a "gladiator" (35). Yet his moral conversion comes about largely because of his commitment to a fertile love for Cherry, whose name suggests the virginal new beginning which their affair represents for both partners.

Both Cherry and Vickie LaMotta (as portrayed by Cathy Moriarty) epitomize the voluptuous blonde to be pursued as part of the American dream. Vickie, from her first introduction to Jake in the movie's pool scene, evokes an intense desirability and personal confidence. As Cis Corman remarks, "Vickie LaMotta had something special...she had an attitude that was extraordinary. It said, 'I'm beautiful, I'm happy, life is joyous... '" (Kelly 131). Cherry is portrayed in her nightclub performance as looking something like Grace Kelly and even like Marilyn Monroe. Rojack tells us, "She looked at different instants like a dozen lovely blondes.... She had studied blondes, this Cherry, she was all of them... " (*Dream* 94-95). Jake's attitude towards Vickie, however, never seems to rise above virulent, self-destructive possessiveness, while Rojack is able to rise above jealousy to a relationship of reciprocal trust with Cherry which strengthens him.

Rojack's continued moral progress may be traced by the strategically placed scenes in which he fights Shago Martin, Cherry's ex-lover, and Barney Oswald Kelly, his evil father-in-law. From Shago he learns mercy when, beaten, the singer says, "I don't hate. Never.... Tell Cherry, her and you, I wish you luck" (183). In his struggle with Kelly, who tries cold-bloodedly to kill him, Rojack uses minimal force and consciously controls his rage, throttling the murderous frenzy he knows himself capable of.

LaMotta, by contrast, chooses violence (admittedly his profession, his route to success) over sexual love, as exemplified in the scene when he extinguishes his lust for Vickie while training for a fight by pouring ice water over his erection. Yet, even in the film's later scenes, the retired and overweight LaMotta is characterized by the barely concealed threat of imminent violence coupled with predatory sexuality that surrounds him like an aura, as in the scene in which he takes marginally unacceptable liberties with the wife (Laura James) of State's Attorney Bronson (D.J. Blair), to whom he is introduced in his night club. A related scene, in which LaMotta permits a fourteen-year-old girl (Mary Albee) to be served alcohol, accepting her lie that she is twenty-one on the evidence of her sophisticated appearance and her kiss, echoes the passage in *An American Dream* when Romeo, upon being introduced to Cherry, kisses her on the mouth and says, "You could charge five bucks for those kisses" (100).

Ultimately, LaMotta is never redeemed to the degree that Rojack is. The extent of his moral change lies primarily in remorse: too little, too late. Even DeNiro, who clearly felt an intense empathy for LaMotta, says simply: "In the end, there was a lot of remorse with Jake, I think—with his brother, his wife...he's sort of stoic. He takes the punishment. He created it, so he has to live with it" (Kelly 143).

LaMotta's story, like Rojack's is peculiarly American, characterized in its early stages by a hunger for fame and material success. Jake's venality is mitigated by his commitment to his chosen profession: he cries after throwing a fight, and displays a religious devotion to his craft, as suggested by the opening credits sequence in which he is shown shadow-boxing in slow motion, alone in a mysteriously shadowy ring, hooded like a monk, to the accompaniment of the ethereal Intermezzo from Pietro Mascagni's *Cavalleria rusticana*. (In the opera itself, the Intermezzo suggests a momentary religious sanctuary before a violent confrontation prompted by jealousy.)

Yet Rojack is more like an American Everyman in that he struggles with fear. In contrast, LaMotta thrives on pain (as we see most dramatically in the scene in which he insists that his brother hit him in the face repeatedly) and ultimately reassesses his life only after his fall from the championship and the failure of his marriage.

Violence is central to both characters, LaMotta and Rojack, the vehicle by which each defines himself. Both *Raging Bull* and *An American Dream* are masterpieces of character study. Ultimately, however, Rojack arrives at a more complete redemption than LaMotta through a profound recognition and redefinition of himself which enables him not only to renounce his rage but to embrace selfless love, Christian mercy and a personal peace beyond that of the raging bull.

Thus, the central difference between Mailer's protagonist and that created by Scorsese and DeNiro is that Rojack, like many characters in Mailer's work, uses his violence to purge his inner corruption and learns, cerebrally and spiritually, to grow beyond it to a true salvation. LaMotta, after the end of his boxing career, is left only with remorse.

CHAPTER 4

THE MYSTERY NOVELS

TOUGH GUYS DON'T DANCE: AN AMERICAN DREAM REVISITED

Mailer's novel *Tough Guys Don't Dance* presents striking parallels to his earlier work *An American Dream*. *Dream* was written hurriedly against monthly deadlines for initial publication in *Esquire* (January through August 1964) and was subsequently adapted for a poor 1966 film starring Stuart Whitman, Eleanor Parker, Lloyd Nolan and Janet Leigh (with which I will deal in detail in Chapter 5). The novel, however, presents many of the significant thematic and symbolic preoccupations that governed Mailer's work for over two decades. These include a highly personal vision of American existentialism, an obsessive preoccupation with cancer as a symbol of moral failure, and above all a Manichaean vision of the universe. *Tough Guys Don't Dance* was written, according to Mailer, in two months. Long sections were excerpted in two issues of *Vanity Fair*, and it was also made into a film, this time under the author's own direction. The later novel is similar to the earlier not only in the circumstances of its composition but also in many of its themes, symbol patterns, and plot situations. Again, an estranged wife is murdered, possibly by her husband, the first-person narrator. Again, the existential will of the protagonist is tested by the danger of falling from heights, by a hostile police investigator, and by various adversaries from the demi-monde. Again, cancer figures prominently, supernatural omens abound, and potential salvation is offered through a regenerative heterosexual love. But unlike *An American Dream*, *Tough Guys Don't Dance* remains merely an entertaining potboiler.

Regarding the circumstances of *Dream's* composition, an interesting if unconvincing case is made by Hershel Parker for the literary superiority of the *Esquire* version over the Dial Press version in *Flawed Texts and Verbal Icons: Literary Authority in American Fiction* (1984). Parker, it must be said, did a difficult and meticulous job of researching and comparing the two. His argument for the primacy of the *Esquire* serial is in no way mean-spirited, nor does it question Mailer's artistic commitment to the book. Nonetheless, I remain convinced that the Dial Press volume, the result of several months of careful revision by the author, is not only the version Mailer wished to publish, but the superior one. Parker, in all fairness, quotes Mailer as saying: "I'm not sure he's [Parker] right. I think the Dial book is better" (Parker 210).

Two primary structural patterns lend coherence to Mailer's thematic preoccupations in *An American Dream*. One is the sense of a pilgrimage by protagonist Stephen Richards Rojack from imminent alcoholism, damnation and madness to salvation and sanity. In a modern analogue of *Pilgrim's Progress*, Rojack confronts a series of adversaries, defeating them and the weaknesses in himself that they represent, and in the process absorbing their strengths. The second is a pattern of sexual connections among the characters, with Rojack at its hub.

In *Cannibals and Christians*, Mailer writes of the sexual nexus in James Baldwin's *Another Country*:

> ... There is a chain of fornication which is all but complete...With the exception of Rufus Scott, who does not go to bed with his sister, everybody else in the book is connected by their skin to another character who is connected to still another.... All the sex in the book is displaced, whites with blacks, men with men, women with homosexuals; the sex is funky to suffocation, rich but claustrophobic, sensual but airless. Baldwin understands the existential abyss of love. In a world of Negroes and whites, nuclear fallout, marijuana, bennies, inversion, insomnia, and tapering off with beer at four in the morning, one no longer falls in love—one has to take a brave leap over the wall of one's impacted rage and cowardice. And nobody makes it, not quite.... They cannot find the juice to break out of their hatred into the other country of love (114).

An American Dream presents a series of characters as promiscuously connected to one another sexually as those who people Baldwin's book. But while the sexual world of Mailer's characters is as dark as the one in *Another Country*, it is also in the realm of sexual love that Mailer presents his statement of hope for salvation; for Rojack and his lover Cherry are ultimately able to take the "brave leap over the wall of...impacted rage and cowardice." So, too, are Tim Madden and Madeleine Falco in *Tough Guys Don't Dance*.

Geometric patterns of sexual connection are central to plot structure and theme in both of the Mailer novels. In *An American Dream*, Rojack is linked to his demonic adversary, Barney Oswald Kelly, by the fact that each has had sexual relations with Deborah, Ruta, and Cherry. In *Tough Guys Don't Dance*, Madden is similarly connected to Meeks Wardley Hilby III through Patty Lareine and to Lonnie Pangborn through Jessica Pond. Madden's most significant connection is to Alvin Luther Regency, the Acting Chief of Police of Provincetown, who has, like Madden, slept with Patty, Madeleine, and even Jessica. Madden finds himself unwittingly participating in a wife-swap with Regency. Unlike the relatively simple, apparently innocent swap twelve years earlier in which Madden met Patty (then married to her first husband, the football coach-preacher-chiropractor called "Big Stoop") and ultimately lost his real love Madeleine, this one has life and death stakes. Madden's parallels to Regency are further emphasized when the latter says, "In my way, I'm a writer too" (228), and when Madden compares himself and Regency to "brothers at odds looking for good marks from our father" (349).

No one and nothing is as it appears to be in *Tough Guys Don't Dance*. Regency, the top police officer, is actually a criminal. The apparent murderer is the only entirely innocent character. The "murdered" wife is actually a murderess until she is herself murdered. Both homosexuals, Wardley and Pangborn, become temporarily heterosexual. The menacing Bolo Green ("Mr. Black"), Patty's chauffeur and lover, becomes affable to Madden (who had been Patty's chauffeur and lover when she was married to Wardley).

A series of minor doppelgangers populates the book, echoing the Madden/Regency connection. Patty and Jessica are so interchangeable as blonde sex objects that Tim is confused as to whose head he first finds in his marijuana stash. Wardley and Pangborn have parallel anomalous sexual relationships with Patty and Jessica respectively (in which they are replaced by Madden) and ultimately shoot themselves with matching pistols. In *An American Dream*, Rojack is linked to adversaries like Roberts, Romeo, Shago, and ultimately Kelly, but repudiates his similarities to them by cleansing his soul of fear in confrontation with them. He is ultimately seen as parallel to Deborah, his murdered wife, by the fact that he, like she, attempts to walk the parapet outside Kelly's Waldorf Towers apartment. But where he succeeds, she has failed. Similarly, Madden is connected to an unlikely counterpart, Hank "Spider" Nissen, by the fact that both made abortive attempts, years apart, to climb the Provincetown Monument. Although he was stopped by the overhang near the top, Tim sees the attempt as beneficial to his soul and his nerve. Spider's serves less purpose, providing him no existential reserve, but merely a parallel which he sordidly emphasizes. As Madden says, "[Spider] would look at me and give a giggle as if we had both had a girl together, and each took turns sitting on her head" (101). And like Madden, Spider is an unsuccessful writer (102), supported by the woman with whom he lives, though Spider and Beth's circumstances are more modest than Tim and Patty's.

If Spider is, in his pinched venality, his vicious treachery, an unlikely alter ego for Madden, Wardley is even more so. Wardley was, surprisingly, a classmate of Madden's at Exeter. Both were expelled on the same day, for different reasons. They were, too, "classmates" at a school of harder knocks: a Florida penitentiary. Further, both have been married to Patty. But the differences between these parallel lives are far more important than their similarities. Wardley is a homosexual by eager and early choice; Madden resists successfully even the enforced homosexuality of the prison power structure. And two instances of appearance masking reality serve finally to define these men. The one redemptive act of courage ever committed by Wardley, the daring creep along a ledge from one window to another of his father's house (though in the service of a venal blackmail scheme), has always elicited from Madden a certain admiration. Madden claims, in fact, that it was this image in his mind that stayed his hand when Patty asked him to kill Wardley. Near the book's conclusion, however, Wardley admits with glee that the story is pure fabrication. And where Madden suspects himself of being Patty's murderer, Wardley reveals that it was in fact he himself. Finally, while Madden goes on to a redemptive new life and love with Madeleine, Wardley shoots himself. Meanwhile, Spider, the other dubious brother of the heights, is revealed as the other half of the Patty-head crime: after Wardley killed her, Spider beheaded her. Wardley in turn killed Spider and buried him near the two headless women.

In *An American Dream*, cancer (in Deborah, Eddie Gannucci, and others) was perceived as a metaphor for a failure of courage. In *Tough Guys Don't Dance*, Patty speaks disdainfully of middle-class kids "[t]rying to get vengeance on their folks for giving them cancer!" (106). More significantly, Dougy Madden, the protagonist's father, presents a cohesive vision of life in which cancer is the eventual consequence of a major failure of will. Ultimately, he forces his own disease into remission through a major act of selfless courage on behalf of his son (sinking the severed heads of Patty and Jessica at sea).

God and the devil are again embattled in a Manichaean struggle over the best and worst in the human soul. Just as Rojack's journey through the New York night and later through the artifice of Las Vegas are seen as infernal, Tim Madden's drive to his marijuana stash where the *heads* are secreted (Mailer may be punning here) smacks of a trip into hell, and provokes an equivalent fear in him. Madden's salvation ultimately must lie in overcoming his visceral fear.

If courage, the capacity to steel oneself and rise above immediate fear, is in *Tough Guys Don't Dance* (as throughout Mailer's work) perceived as the noblest expression of the *human* will, many of the characters are described in pointedly animal terms. Madden, two-thirds of the way up the Provincetown Monument, unable to proceed or retreat, feels "like a cat trapped for six days in a tree" (99). Alone at night, fearing unknown adversaries, he says "panic soiled me. I was like a puppy in a new house" (75). And facing a new challenge, Madden feels "a descent from man to dog" (97) before he musters the will to go on. Yet, ironically, the attributes of a true dog are positive. Tim's Labrador Retriever, "Stunts" (so named because of his inability to learn any), demonstrates courage, sacrifice, and loyalty when he gives his life for Madden, dying with Spider's knife in his heart. The truly negative animal metaphors are reserved for Spider himself, in his hideous nickname, his "crablike mouth" (103) and in Madden's observation that "he had a touch of the hyena…that same we-eat-tainted-meat-together intimacy that burns out of a hyena's eyes behind the bars of his cage" (101).

In *Tough Guys Don't Dance*, Bolo Green ("Mr. Black"), Patty's lover, has eyes like a lion (219). He is clearly parallel to Cherry's lover, Shago Martin, in *An American Dream*, even to the detail that in their confrontations with these black sexual rivals, Madden and Rojack see the light in the room turn literally red (*Tough Guys* 220; *American Dream* 192) with tension and rage. Like another Rojack adversary, Romeo Romalozzo, Bolo is an ex-boxer.

It is Dougy Madden for whom the most positive animal imagery is reserved. He has "tiger's balls" (254) and is "powerful as a Kodiak bear" (88), descriptions which emphasize his massive size and courage, and his large role as a touchstone or paradigm for his son.

In fact, it was Dougy who provided Tim with the veritable Zen koan which forms the title of this book: *Tough Guys Don't Dance* (originated by another fighter, Rocky Graziano). Even in the modest lesson of the boxing anecdote that provides this title, Mailer shows less thematic ambition than in the earlier title, *An American Dream*, with its enormous reverberations.

Despite the mixed reviews and critical controversy which its publication engendered, *An American Dream* has generally enjoyed a gathering approval from critics. On the front page of the *New York Times Book Review*, Joan Didion wrote:

> ... he has written [the] "big book" at least three
> times now. He wrote it the first time in 1955
> with *The Deer Park* and *he wrote it a second
> time in 1965 with An American Dream* and he
> wrote it a third time in 1967 with *Why Are We
> in Vietnam?*...[my italics]

The equivalent certainly cannot be claimed for *Tough
Guys Don't Dance*. Even Mailer's plans for it were rather modest. Long after its publication, he was quoted in the *Philadelphia Inquirer* Sunday magazine as saying:

> This book is like an illegitimate baby. It was
> written in two months, therefore born out of
> wedlock, and I'm struck by the fact that the
> event took place.... I couldn't write a word
> for months and had been drawing an advance... if I didn't write it, with all I owed the
> IRS and my old publisher, I'd have to begin
> cheating Random House immediately... (40).

After various disclaimers and qualifications, he continued:

> I'd been thinking of doing [a murder mystery]
> for many years. And I've always loved
> Hammett and Chandler. Whenever I get tired
> of writing, I go and read them. I read them
> five times, eight times. Every one of their
> books. This is over many years, over 40 years.
> They're a tonic. So, I've always wanted to write

a murder mystery, and I've always been very curious as to how it would turn out (44).

He concluded:

I realized after a while that, for me, knowing what the plot of my book was going to be in detail would be like being married to someone whose every habit you knew. And there was just no life left in the relationship. And there's something stifling about a book whose end appears to me immediately. I prefer to discover the end of a book (44).

This attitude may finally be the key to the differences in scope and quality between the two books.

In *An American Dream*, the numerous apparent coincidences are explained in terms of a cohesive cosmic order within which Mailer's God and Devil struggle for men's souls, the concept of "an architecture to eternity" dealt with in Chapter 2, above.

But in *Tough Guys Don't Dance*, the series of murders and beheadings, when revealed, are reminiscent of Elizabethan blood tragedy. Stated in bald outline, they seem almost silly: There are seven deaths (five murders and two suicides) and two post-mortem beheadings, perpetrated by many different culprits. It is as though Mailer is just having fun with the reader, toying with the genre. In *An American Dream*, Mailer took a cliché (as indicated by his title) and made of it an allegorical indictment of American society. In *Tough Guys Don't Dance*, he takes a potentially serious popular form and in a

good-natured and unpretentious, if bloody, manner, makes a
cliché of it.

Ultimately, the primary difference between these two
novels is apparent in their respective conclusions. *An American Dream* ends on a sophisticated series of controlled ambiguities, which is to say that there is a *resolution* of Rojack's
existential quest, but no simple final *solutions* to the various
mysteries presented in the course of it. What was Jack
Kennedy's true connection to Kelly? Was Deborah really a spy,
or even a double agent? What was the nature of the "work"
Cherry once did for Detective Roberts? It does not, finally,
matter, any more than it matters whether Hawthorne's Young
Goodman Brown was or wasn't dreaming, or what the minister's
black veil really stood for. A literal explanation of these interesting ambiguities would render the story pedestrian, rob it of
nuance.

Tough Guys Don't Dance, on the other hand, ends on a
lengthy series of elaborate, often forced explanations of how
various culprits and an additional supporting cast did away
with the seven victims. There are solutions in abundance, but
no true *resolution*, and Madden's new beginning with his old
love, Madeleine, is a pallid echo of Rojack's discovery of love
with Cherry.

Perhaps Madden's return to Madeleine may serve as a
metaphor for Mailer's return to his old love for the mystery
novel in an attempt to replicate his daring success in *An American Dream*. But as Mailer said of his early work *Barbary Shore*
in *Advertisements for Myself* (91-94), *Tough Guys Don't Dance*
collapses in its last hundred pages, and never recovers.

CHAPTER 5

TOUGH GUY GOES HOLLYWOOD: MAILER AND THE MOVIES

Norman Mailer's relationship with the world of film has grown throughout his career from passive and distant to active and quite intimate. The earliest adaptations of his work—the movie versions of *The Naked and the Dead* (1958) and *An American Dream* (1966)—are quite awful. While both films have many weaknesses, the primary failure in each case lies in the respective conclusions, which dramatically reverse Mailer's intended vision.

In *The Naked and the Dead* (novel), the liberal, Harvard-educated Lieutenant Hearn struggles politically and metaphysically with the conservative General Cummings, while the malevolent Sergeant Croft plots to regain control of Hearn's platoon. One of Mailer's primary thematic messages in the novel involves the collusion of Croft with Martinez to withhold information which ultimately results in Hearn's death. Thus, on an allegorical level, Mailer forcefully suggests that postwar American liberalism will be destroyed by the uneasy alliance of the upper and lower classes in their affinity for reactionary political views. The movie version of *The Naked and the Dead*, however, is a wretched distortion. Sergeant Croft (played by Aldo Ray) is killed by Japanese fire, while Lieutenant Hearn (Cliff Robertson) is wounded but carried safely back to head-quarters by the enlisted men of his platoon, notably "a Baptist preacher and a wandering Jew," thus thwarting the tyrannical fascist General Cummings (Raymond Massey). In fact, in the screenplay by Denis and Terry Sanders, Robertson's Hearn tri-umphantly announces to Massey's Cummings, "There is a spirit in man that will survive...godlike, eternal, indestructible."

In Mailer's *An American Dream*, the existential and ul-timately hopeful vision of the novel is implicit in the fact that Stephen Richards Rojack survives the horrific American expe-rience, aided by the sacrificial deaths of his lover Cherry and her ex-lover, the black jazz musician Shago Martin. In the movie (whose title in British release was *See You in Hell, Darling*), Rojack (Stuart Whitman) is killed by mobsters after being be-trayed by Cherry (Janet Leigh), who thus saves herself. The last line in the movie is her solitary murmur: "What did you expect from a whore?" Shago (Paul Mantee) is present for only a brief moment. Thus, Mailer's indictment of the flaws and hypocrisies endemic in American society, coupled with exis-tential hope and expressed so powerfully in the novel, is re-placed in the film by a general sense of purposeless cynicism; and the novel's allegorical implication that what is potentially fine in the American character can best be realized by an alli-ance with subjugated groups like blacks and women is completely lost on the screen.

During the late 1960s, Mailer's relationship with movies took a new turn: he produced, directed and starred in three
feature-length films—*Wild 90* (1967), the story of three gang-
sters in hiding; *Beyond the Law* (1968), set in a police station
during a series of interrogations; and most notoriously,
Maidstone (1971), a mystery involving an assassination attempt
upon a presidential candidate/film director, Norman T. Kingsley
(played by Norman Kingsley Mailer). Made with no script, no
retakes, and no continuity ("Everything…is created as he cuts,"
noted Sally Beauman in an essay excerpted in the book version of *Maidstone* [9]), these unconventional productions were
critical and financial failures, though Mailer demonstrated a
gathering understanding and control of cinematic technique
with each one. When *Maidstone* was issued as a paperback
book in 1971, Mailer added an essay on filmmaking in which,
among other things, he contemplated the difficulty of "trans-
porting a novelist's vision of life over to a film" (143) and concluded that, since the coherence of the original novel is "cre-
mated and strewn" by the process of adaptation, it is "no wonder great novels invariably make the most disappointing
movies,…and modest novels…sometimes make very good
movies" (144). A decade later, in 1981, he returned to Hollywood in yet another role: a convincing cameo appearance as
Stanford White in the movie version of E. L. Doctorow's *Ragtime*, directed by Milos Forman.

Also in 1981, Mailer wrote the screenplay for the 1982
NBC Television miniseries based on his 1979 "true life novel,"
The Executioner's Song, which was later shown on cable pre-
mium channels and seen in theaters in Europe. Mailer was
nominated for an Emmy award for the screenplay, and Tommy

Lee Jones won one (Outstanding Actor in a Drama Special) for his starring role as Gary Gilmore, the first man to be executed in America in ten years. So eager was Mailer to write this screenplay himself that he took the unusual step of writing on speculation. The fact that this was clearly a labor of love shows in the vitality of the production, which garnered generally strong reviews. Subsequently, Mailer explained, "I thought no one could do 'The Executioner's Song' as well as I could. Part of the problem is that it's a very long book with over 200 characters, and a job of digestion had to be done. I wrote that book, so I'd already done that digesting" (Harmetz C8).

But the most important film of Mailer's career to date is unquestionably *Tough Guys Don't Dance*, based on his 1984 novel of the same title, for which Mailer wrote the screenplay and also directed. *Tough Guys* is the story of Tim Madden—ex-con, ex-amateur fighter, and unsuccessful writer—who wakes up with a hangover one morning to discover a new tattoo on his arm, a fresh blood stain on his car seat, and a severed head in his marijuana stash. Although Tim has only vague memories of his activities during the previous night, he begins to fear his complicity in the various murders which are soon revealed; and he tries to reconstruct the events so that he can prove his innocence to himself and to those who suspect him.

Ironically, *Tough Guys*, a far less ambitious novel than *Dream*, becomes in Mailer's hands a far more artistically successful film. As both screenwriter and director, he manages to translate to the screen much of the tonal ambience of the novel's fictive voice, as integral to his work as Fitzgerald's finely styled narrative is to *The Great Gatsby*. But whereas *Gatsby's* tonal resonance is lost and the awkwardness of the bald plot made prominent (despite Nick Carraway's verbatim voice-over in the third film adaptation), Mailer as director is able to evoke even more fully than he did in his novel the bleakness of his Provincetown winter; and while his adaptation of *Tough Guys* still highlights (as in the *Gatsby* films) the excesses of the murder mystery plot, they are ameliorated to some degree by a pervasive tone of black humor.

I have already dealt with the circumstances under which Mailer wrote the novel *Tough Guys*, and the fact that the mystery was a form to which he had been drawn for some time. Although the novel is overshadowed by the works which precede and follow it, notably *Ancient Evenings*, which it most immediately follows, *An American Dream*, which it most closely resembles, and *Harlot's Ghost* (1991), which dwarfs most of his previous works, its themes and situations are classic Mailer. Here again are the progressively more refined symbolic preoccupations that have governed his work for decades: existentialism, cancer and Manichaeism. I have earlier (in Chapter 4) noted the echoes of *American Dream* in the plot of *Tough Guys*.

The primary structural patterns which lend coherence to Mailer's themes in both novels are the pilgrimages of Rojack and Madden to redemption, and the network of sexual connections among the characters, with these protagonists at their respective centers. These structural devices are replicated in both versions of *Tough Guys Don't Dance*. If, in both novels, the series of sexual links among the characters suggests an apparent cynicism, it is nonetheless by virtue of love that Mailer offers the possibility of hope, for Tim Madden and Madeleine Falco (like Rojack and Cherry in *American Dream*) are ultimately able, in both versions of *Tough Guys*, to find the courage to make a new beginning.

Mailer's protagonist, the aspiring novelist Tim Mad-

den (in the film, surprisingly well-evoked in his seedy alcoholism by Ryan O'Neal), lies at the center of this complex round
of sexual connections. Tim is connected to his former prep
school classmate, multimillionaire Meeks Wardley Hilby III
(called Wardley Meeks III in the film and played by John
Bedford Lloyd) through Tim's estranged wife Patty Lareine
(Debra Sandlund), and to Meeks' associate, Lonnie Pangborn
(R. Patrick Sullivan) through Jessica Pond (Frances Fisher),
whom Tim meets—and sleeps with—on the fateful night he
does not fully recall. But Madden's most significant connection is to Alvin Luther Regency (Wings Hauser), the Acting
Chief of Police of Provincetown, who, like Madden, has been
intimate with Patty Lareine and Jessica Pond and who is married to Tim's former lover, Madeleine Falco (Isabella Rossellini).

Wings Hauser is quite effective at portraying Regency's
intense rectitude (echoed in his middle name, "Luther") as
well as his criminal venality, his sexual rapacity and his borderline madness. (He sometimes looks as if he is about to ro-
tate his head 360 degrees and vomit pea soup.) In fact, he tells
Tim and his father, Dougy, that he has two sides, "the enforcer
and the maniac."

These geometric sexual patterns in turn are part of a
series of shifting criminal alliances and betrayals which lead
in the book to five murders and two suicides (six and one in
the film), and two post-mortem beheadings, treated with a
more disarming black humor in the film's conclusion than in
the novel. Yet the most significant relationship in both versions is that between Tim and his forceful father Dougy, powerfully portrayed by Lawrence Tierney, an actor who in life
had a history of drunken brawling similar to that of his character, which kept him unemployable for many years. Tierney

maintains that his career was sabotaged by gossip columnist Hedda Hopper, who would "print terrible lies" about him (Peary 104). Most of his early roles were as criminals in 1940s B-movies, including *Dillinger* (1945) and *Born to Kill* (1947). He also played Jesse James in *Badman's Territory* (1946) and *Best of the Badmen* (1951), and the villain who "derailed the circus train in Cecil B. DeMille's *The Greatest Show on Earth* (1952)" (Peary 104-7). After Tierney quit drinking, he played in *Prizzi's Honor* (1985) and appeared in episodes of *Hill Street Blues* as, ironically, a police sergeant. It is Dougy who provides the book's title, although the boxing anecdote is omitted from the film; it is Dougy who, despite being ravaged by cancer, remains the tough guy, though he confesses that the spirits now hover about him at night and taunt him, telling him it is time for him to dance; and it is Dougy who performs the dirtier responsibilities, such as disposing of the severed heads, which Tim cannot. In a nice symmetry at the end of the film, however, Dougy (made a little less tough by his illness) and Tim (made a little more tough by his recent experience) work together to clean up the week's horrific mess when they sail out at night and dispose of the bodies.

As in the novel, one aspect of this father-son bond is evoked when Tim reassures Dougy, who has worried that Tim's mother's "delicacy" may have been passed on to his son, that he has refused to acquiesce to sexual intimidation in prison. "They called me Iron Jaw" (254), he tells Dougy in the novel; in the film his declaration becomes, "I did three years in the slammer standing up. Nobody made a punk out of me."

Many of the differences between the film and the novel versions of *Tough Guys Don't Dance* are implicit in the respective strengths and limitations of the two media. It is obvious that Mailer was obliged to telescope various events and limit or cut scenes or characters in order to fit the several hundred pages into two hours. Examples include the omission of minor characters like the eccentric local Harpo, nicknamed for his desire to "harpoon" women; in the novel Harpo does Tim's new tattoo, while in the movie that task falls to Spider's accomplice, Stoodie. Bolo Green (played by Clarence Williams III of *Mod Squad* infamy) disappears after the first scene, and the plot is altered so that his murder of Stoodie is committed by Wardley. The motives for most of the murders and beheadings are ascribed almost entirely to greed over a proposed cocaine deal, with dashes of lust and jealousy (notably in Patty Lareine's murder of Jessica Pond), whereas in the novel much of the plot involves a real estate scam.

Several of the symbol patterns in the novel are, of necessity, omitted or deemphasized in the film. The animal imagery is cut, so that although John Snyder's portrayal of Spider Nissen in the film evokes a palpable distaste in the viewer, his hyena-like quality is only vaguely implied. The appearance of Tim's dog "Stunts" to sacrifice his life for Tim is sudden and unexpected. The doppleganger pattern is minimized so that Spider's shared experiences with Tim (notably the failed attempt to climb the Provincetown monument) are deleted, the confusion over whose head first appears in Tim's marijuana stash is negligible, and Wardley and Pangborn do not both commit suicide with matching pistols. Instead, Pangborn is shot by Jessica, who uses the pistol he has foolishly handed over to her.

While all of the aforementioned changes are explicable, even expected, there are two striking alterations—in point of view and in the film's conclusion—which profoundly alter the thematic message of the work. The almost complete loss of Tim Madden's first person narrative and his concomitant internal cerebrations weaken the film somewhat, since Tim's existential struggles with his own fears (as in the case of scaling the monument) are omitted or less effectively evoked. This is evident at its most awkward in the scene when Tim, confronted by Madeleine's note informing him that her husband Regency and Tim's wife Patty are having an affair, repeats the seemingly interminable litany, "Oh God, Oh man," as the sky wheels about him.

Mailer addressed the issue of point of view directly in an interview with Dinitia Smith for *New York* magazine:

> It's difficult not entering Madden's head. There's no offscreen narration. Narration in a film is a confession of weakness. Offscreen narration ruined *Sunset Boulevard* and *Apocalypse Now*. The more sardonic aspects of Madden's character can hardly be captured (Smith 32).

Mailer does, however, bring the illusion and flavor of the first person narrative into the early stages of the movie by the common and simple expedient of having Tim relate the story to date to his father: awakening on the 28th day of Patty's "decampment" to find Dougy seated at the table in his dining room, Tim recounts the strange happenings of the past week. And ultimately, Mailer added a Madden voice-over before the final cut.

In the novel, after a series of somewhat improbable resolutions (or simple solutions) to the involved plot, Tim and Madeleine move to Key West, living modestly both in terms of finances and hopes:

> Madeleine and I went out to Colorado for a
> while, and now we inhabit Key West. I try to
> write, and we live on the money that comes
> from her work as a hostess in a local restau-
> rant and mine as a part-time bartender in a
> hole across the street from her place. Once in
> a while we wait for a knock on the door, but I
> am not so sure it will ever come (*Tough Guys*
> 367).

Thus, Tim and Madeleine find themselves in similar,
if slightly more modest and certainly more satisfying, circumstances to those they lived in at the beginning of their affair
years earlier.

In the screenplay, however, Madeleine surprises Tim
with a house, presumably in Key West, purchased with the
two million dollars from the aborted coke deal which precipi-
tates most of the murders, money which she found in a brief-
case in Regency's closet. Her final line—and the final line in
the film—is "Carry me across the threshold, you dummy." In
terms of verisimilitude, it may be remarked that two people
appearing so suddenly and acquiring their home so mysteriously would seem quite obtrusive. But Mailer's intent here may
be part of the borderline parody and consequent black humor
of the film's concluding messages, which make the film's ending superior to the book's: we have just witnessed Dougy and
Tim sinking six bodies at sea while "Pomp and Circumstance"
plays in the background and they discuss cancer and schizo-
phrenia as mutual cures. In the novel, Mailer writes, "Doubt-

less I am in danger of writing an Irish comedy, so I will not describe the gusto with which Dougy now made his preparations to take Alvin Luther to the watery rest… " (367). In the movie, he makes us witnesses to the act itself. Perhaps because of this ameliorating shift to sardonic humor, the film's excesses are more acceptable than those of the novel, since the audience's expectations of verisimilitude are minimized.

Mailer apparently enjoyed bringing his novel to the screen. He spent six months on the screenplay (compared to only two months for the writing of the book on which it is based); and, as he remarked to me and to other interviewers, he liked the excitement involved in directing, especially after decades of writing in isolation: "I enjoyed it a lot. The trouble is, I like making movies more than writing now. I'm tired of writing. I've been doing it for forty years, and there's not much fun left" (Leeds, "Conversation," 6-7). (This attitude, by the evidence, was to change with the massive achievement of his next novel, *Harlot's Ghost*.) Furthermore, in addition to directing the film, throughout the production he engaged himself personally in other ways: it is his Provincetown home—radically redecorated, with white lacquer and pastel colors in keeping with Patty Lareine's social aspirations—which serves as Tim and Patty's Provincetown residence; and according to the credits, Mailer even co-authored the lyrics to one of the film's songs, "You'll Come Back (You Always Do)." There was also a special kinship with some of the actors: Ryan O'Neal was an old sparring buddy, whose reputation for bellicosity rivals Mailer's. And Mailer's fifth wife, Carol Stevens, played the voice of one of the witches.

The film *Tough Guys Don't Dance* was met with sometimes negative or hostile reviews. But despite the criticism,

Mailer in his first foray as director of a major commercial film shows his growth and virtuosity as an artist, and presents us with precisely what he described in *Maidstone*: a good movie from a modest novel.

CHAPTER 6

HARLOT'S GHOST: YET ANOTHER BIG BOOK

In 1959, Norman Mailer aired an ambition in *Advertisements for Myself* which he must have known (and intended) that the literary world would never let him forget: to "try to hit the longest ball ever to go up into the accelerated hurricane air of our American letters" (477).

Since then, Mailer has written many books, several of them massive in size and scope, which his detractors have rejected as failed attempts to fulfill this promise. Joan Didion described this critical phenomenon best in the *New York Times Book Review*, when in writing of *The Executioner's Song* she forcefully insisted:

> It is one of those testimonies to the tenacity of self-regard in the literary life that large numbers of people remain persuaded that Norman Mailer is no better than their reading of him.

They condescend to him, they dismiss his
most original work in favor of the more literal
and predictable rhythms of *The Armies of the
Night*; they regard *The Naked and the Dead* as
a promise later broken and every book since
as a quick turn for his creditors, a stalling action, a spangled substitute, tarted up to de-
ceive, for the "big book" he cannot write. In
fact, he has written this "big book" at least
three times now. He wrote it the first time in
1955 with *The Deer Park* and he wrote it a
second time in 1965 with *An American Dream*
and he wrote it a third time in 1967 with *Why
Are We in Vietnam?* and now, with *The
Executioner's Song*, he has probably written it
a fourth (1).

Now comes *Harlot's Ghost*, another "big book" (1310
pages), which, following such cinder-block sized works as
Executioner's Song and *Ancient Evenings,* gives the lie yet again
to such caviling critics.

What can one say about *Harlot's Ghost* that hasn't already been said in the virtual ream of reviews, the mass media
articles about its publication, the videotape library of interviews with its author, who at age 68 showed signs of mellow-
ing but not of slowing down? Plenty. For one thing, except for
brief and generally facile allusions to a few earlier works, no
one, with the possible exception of Michael Glenday in *Norman
Mailer* (1995), has explored the extent to which this novel is
profoundly rooted in the recurrent thematic preoccupations
of Mailer's enormous body of work, spanning half a century, at

the same time that it takes them a leap forward and breaks new artistic ground.

To begin with, the relationship between the protagonist, Herrick (Harry/Rick) Hubbard—from his privileged boarding school and Yale education to his lifetime career in the CIA—with his godfather and mentor, the titular "Harlot" (a CIA cryptonym for Hugh Tremont Montague) echoes several earlier tutor/tyro relationships. These range from the problematic and sexually colored connection of General Cummings and Lieutenant Robert Hearn in *The Naked and the Dead* through the more benign influences of McLeod upon Mikey Lovett in *Barbary Shore* and Charles Eitel on Sergius O'Shaugnessy in *The Deer Park* to the insidious temptation of Stephen Rojack by Barney Oswald Kelly in *An American Dream*.

Again, the new departure which marks one of the virtues of *Tough Guys Don't Dance* is that Mailer created a moving father/son relationship between Tim Madden and his memorable and larger-than-life father, Dougy. This is echoed in Harry's growing emotional ties to his father, Boardman Kimball (Cal) Hubbard (a.k.a. Halifax). As a second generation CIA agent and nth generation patrician, Harry is quite different from Tim Madden, as his father is quite different intellectually from Dougy, the huge, rough-hewn barkeeper. Yet the similarities are more profound and telling than the superficial differences. Both sons ultimately gain the love and approval of their fathers by means of resourcefulness, courage and force of will rather than more abstract or intellectual capabilities.

Finally, the problematic and often adversarial friendship between Harry and his fellow CIA classmate, the terrifying Dix Butler, prompts comparison to that of D.J., narrator/

protagonist of *Why Are We in Vietnam?* and his best friend Tex Hyde, Sergius and Marion Faye in *Deer Park*, and to a lesser degree Tim Madden and Spider Nissen in *Tough Guys*. Like these pairs, Dix and Harry are alter egos, virtual doppelgangers, and like them, there is an ambivalent attraction between the two.

Dix Butler is really scary. He would clearly prove more than a match for such earlier sociopaths in Mailer's work and real life as Sergeant Sam Croft (*Naked*), Chief of Police Alvin Regency (*Tough Guys*), Gary Gilmore, and perhaps even Jack Henry Abbott. Capable of the most barbaric cruelties, he illuminates and foregrounds the ethical conflicts to which Harry Hubbard makes us privy in himself.

If these parallels appear to be common Mailer currency, another which is definitely of more recent vintage is an echo of *Ancient Evenings*: Early in *Harlot's Ghost*, having survived a near-fatal skid on an icy road, Harry wonders seriously whether he is actually dead, his body back in his crumpled car, while his mind, still alive for a brief period, seems to be experiencing the terrifying events that follow, just as Menenhetet II in the early pages of *Ancient Evenings* comes to realize that he is indeed dead but still conscious, his soul alive and ambulatory.

Although these analogues within the body of Mailer's work begin to suggest that the armature of *Harlot's Ghost* is formed of the male relationships of which Harry Hubbard is the hub, at least two more primary patterns form this core. One is the series of heterosexual relationships in Harry's life, notably those with his wife, Kittredge, and with Modene Murphy—mistress to John Kennedy, Mafia boss Sam Giancana, Frank Sinatra, and Harry Hubbard—a character partially modeled on Judith Exner. The third is Harry's development through apprenticeship to full-fledged maturity as a CIA operative, and his concurrent development as a man, through the various moral and physical tests of his courage that color and inform Harry's largely epistolary account of his life.

Hadley Kittredge Gardiner Montague Hubbard, wife sequentially to Harlot and Harry, is first of all cast in literary terms. She is named after Hadley Richardson, Hemingway's first wife, and her father is a pompous "Harvard professor of a variety that may no longer exist" (166), who is not only a Shakespearean but distantly related to George Lyman Kittredge. Upon their first meeting, Harry describes her as follows: "She could have been a heroine out of her father's collection of painted Victorian damsels, pale as their cloisters, lovely as angels" (167-68). Subsequently Kittredge remarks, "'I believe Daddy thinks of me as Desdemona'" (168). When she kisses Harry for the first time, he compares the experience to reading the first sentence of *Moby-Dick* (172).

One of Kittredge's primary contributions to the novel is her elaborate Alpha/Omega theory, as explained at length in her letters to Harry (175). To simplify dramatically, Alpha/Omega as advanced by Kittredge not only fits predictably into the pattern of distinct (if often complex) polarities which form the warp and woof of Mailer's thought; it also announces a new, sympathetic and resonant awareness of human androgyny, analogous to that courageously attempted by Hemingway in *The Garden of Eden*.

If there is a primary theme which is utterly central to Mailer's life and work, it is the existential definition of self through overcoming physical as well as moral challenges, learning to control and surmount one's fears. In *Harlot's*

Ghost, the paradigm for this occurs quite early, when Harlot takes the seventeen-year-old Harry rock-climbing for the first time. Frightened by the heights, but more afraid of disgracing himself before his godfather, Harry succeeds and learns a lesson about the nature of fear and courage: "I was commencing to learn that fear was a ladder whose rungs are surmounted one by one, and at the summit—as Mr. Montague would probably say—lay Judgement itself" (150). The quotation is itself a direct reprise of Mailer's statement in *The Armies of the Night*:

> Seen from one moral position...prison could be nothing but an endless ladder of moral challenges. Each time you climbed a step... another higher, more dangerous...step would present itself.... One ejected oneself from guilt by climbing the ladder—the first step back, no matter where, offered nothing but immersion into nausea (195).

The particular challenge to one's courage presented by ascending heights looks back to the climbing of Mount Anaka by Croft's platoon in *The Naked and the Dead*, to Tim Madden's attempt to climb the Provincetown Monument in *Tough Guys Don't Dance*, and most importantly to Rojack's emblematic struggle toward overcoming his fear on the parapet in *An American Dream*. Mailer himself confessed in *The Fight* to his personal habit—one he was trying to break—of walking parapets.

In fact, if there is one work to which *Harlot's Ghost* looks back persistently, it is *An American Dream*: its Manichaean polarities; its interlocking sexual linkage; its references to John F. Kennedy, the CIA, the labyrinthine convolutions of clandestine international politics; above all, its concern with the existential responsibility of the individual to grow in moral stature. Even in many particulars, *Harlot* echoes or replicates details of *Dream*. "Deep Purple" (493) is the theme music which plays just before Harry begins his affair with Sally Porringer, as it was just before Rojack's with Cherry. Harry is conscious of the fact that he is part Jewish, as is Rojack. Harlot and Harry are linked sexually through Kittredge, as Rojack and Kelly were through Cherry, Ruta and Deborah. Dix Butler believes firmly in his own telepathic and telekinetic powers, as does Rojack. Again, Dix's offer of homosexual union to Harry (324-25) in which the latter rejects the enormous temptation to "steal something of his strength" (325) replicates the Tex and D.J. scene in *Vietnam* as well as the Shago Martin and Barney Oswald Kelly passages of *American Dream*. The latter parallel is fleshed out a few pages later when, the same night he has rejected anal sex with Dix, Harry experiences his first vaginal intercourse with Ingrid (329), the polarity of the two echoing the crucial Ruta passage that establishes the Manichaean duality of *Dream*. Even the setting (Berlin), the imagery and odors— "A thin avaricious smell certainly came up from her, single-minded as a cat… " (329)— recall Ruta: "She [Ruta] made the high nasal sound of a cat disturbed in its play…" (*Dream* 45). Harry's frightening mock interrogation during CIA training at the hands of bullying agents in East German uniforms (217ff) has elements of Detective Roberts questioning Rojack, as well as Alvin Regency grilling Tim Madden in *Tough Guys* and the FBI agents browbeating Sergius O'Shaugnessy in *Deer Park*.

Cal is reminiscent of Rojack in that during World War II he killed five German soldiers within three days, a central experience of his life which gave him "a private sense of empowerment, and a great worry on occasion that [he is] mad" (1237). And Cal tells Harry on another occasion of strangling a partisan traitor and the consequent "sense of re-alization you can get killing another human, I mean that intimately" (830).

Not many books have gotten more ink than *Harlot's Ghost*, but then not many have given more ink (1310 pages). Perhaps most interesting are the responses of its subjects. As reported by Elaine Sciolino in the *New York Times* (2 Feb. 1992), an audience of more than five hundred CIA agents met with Mailer in a spirit of remarkable mutual affability, although they were pleased to point out inaccuracies in the novel. Said Mailer of his audience, "If I was told I was in a seminar at Georgetown or Harvard where intelligence was being discussed, I wouldn't think twice." One official responded, "What did he expect? Guys with guns?" More specifically, E. Howard Hunt, who figures largely as a character in the novel, wrote of the novel in *GQ*: "The writer who presumes to reveal the inner world of espionage without having experienced it is comparable to a young man haunting a brothel exit and asking patrons what it was like" (qtd. in Sciolino).

Other characters from real life are more significant since they represent touchstones throughout much of Mailer's work. These are John F. Kennedy and Marilyn Monroe. *An American Dream* begins: "I met Jack Kennedy in November, 1946" (9). *The Presidential Papers* offered the young president advice on running the country. In *Harlot*, Harry Hubbard, rather than going on a double date with the young congressman Kennedy as Rojack had, actually competes with him for the sexual favors and love of Modene Murphy (834, 895 ff). Seeing the president from a distance at the Orange Bowl, Harry remarks:

> … the situation was bizarre. I was looking at Modene's ex-lover. He was the one who finally had not wanted her all that much. Since she, somewhat earlier, had not wanted me, I had to wonder if I was the only man in all of the Orange Bowl who had such an unhappy if intimate purchase on the presidency (1159).

And his identification and competition with JFK is illuminated by the perception that Jackie Kennedy looks like Kittredge in his mind's eye (970). In fact, though Harry never actually meets Jack Kennedy, the President does meet and charm Kittredge, who is briefly an accessory to his affair with one of her friends. Kennedy's assassination, as in real life, is shrouded in ambiguity. Harry concludes:

> I was at the point where I was ready to believe that Allen Dulles did it. Or Harlot. Or, in the great net of implication, Cal and I might be guilty as well. Thoughts raced. I had not yet approached my first piece of universal wisdom: There are no answers—there are only questions.
>
> Of course, some questions have to be better than others (1265).

A similar ambiguity surrounds Marilyn Monroe's death as dealt with in *Harlot's Ghost*. After Mailer's perceptive (if obsessive) preoccupation with and theorizing over Marilyn's life and death in *Marilyn*, *Of Women and Their Elegance* and "Strawhead," it comes as no surprise that he treats her with the same sense of mystery here. Cal goes so far as to suspect the Kennedys and then to conclude instead that Jimmy Hoffa had Monroe murdered to cast suspicion on Bobby and Jack (1239-41). In his Author's Note at the conclusion of *Harlot*, Mailer writes: "… it is the author's contention that good fiction—if the writer can achieve it—is more real, that is, more nourishing to our sense of reality, than nonfiction… " (1287-88). To my mind, Mailer has succeeded in writing a book as nourishing as a thirteen course meal.

Harlot's Ghost looks back to the themes, even the situations, of his earlier books, primarily *An American Dream*, which I believe to be the key to his most fully realized works of the past quarter century. What, then, is it that makes this novel significant? The answer lies in the fact that Mailer's work is fugue-like, an ongoing score in developing counterpoint, which works, reworks and advances to greater maturity the force and cohesion of his omnifarious perceptions of our society and the human condition. More specifically, the novel's fundamental themes are identity and American society, especially in the years 1945 to 1965.

Yet I sense, as I conclude, that certain structural problems in *Harlot's Ghost* are troubling, and perhaps contagious. When he was informed that if the novel went beyond its current length it could not be bound by means of existing technology, Mailer brought the book to a somewhat truncated conclusion, leaving the resolution of the suspenseful frame story for a sequel. I see now that it is appropriate that I end this chapter, as he did the book, with the words:

TO BE CONTINUED

CHAPTER 7

A CONVERSATION WITH NORMAN MAILER

BARRY LEEDS: May I call you Norman?

NORMAN MAILER: Sure, no problem.

LEEDS: I asked you that years ago, but I didn't know if you remembered or not. I don't like just taking those liberties. One of the things that impressed me very much was when I saw you on TV with Henry Miller. You were no kid at the time, but you said, "May I call you Henry, Mr. Miller?" in an era when aluminum siding salesmen call up and say, "Hey, Barry boy, how you doin'." [laughter]...I was rereading *The Fight* just the other day, and I enjoyed yet again that scene where you're running with Ali, especially when you're coming back by yourself and the lion roars. I love that part. I've quoted that to about fifty people.

MAILER: Yeah. I remember George Plimpton wrote about it and got it all wrong.

LEEDS: Well, I hope you got everything right about

him in *The Fight*. By the way, now that it's pretty well documented that Ali has been damaged by boxing, do you love the sport as much as you did?

MAILER: Well, I don't think I love it as much as I used to. One reason is because he's out of it.

LEEDS: Right.

MAILER: In the beginning it's dull drunks with fight reporters, who are pretty simple-minded people, and you chew the fight to bits before it takes place, and everybody's got a theory, and of course half the theories automatically end up being wrong, and even the half that are right are usually misplaced to a degree, and then two out of three fights aren't that good, so you end up saying how many weeks do I have to do this? And you have to write about it afterward. The fight itself, a big championship fight, can still be about the most exciting spectacle in all the world. But the odds are poor. Maybe you get one out of four.

LEEDS: One of the things that struck me the other day, for what it's worth, is something out of my own life. About a hundred years ago, when I was a sixteen-year-old merchant seaman and high school dropout, I worked under a bosun who had an interesting set of literary criteria. He said, "I read a lot of books, but not unless they got fightin' and fuckin' in them," and that seemed reasonable to me at the time. I didn't ask him if he read your books because who was I—I couldn't spell Norman Mailer at the time. But in a sense, it's this violence and sex in your work for which it's been attacked by some critics that in a way led me back into the world of literature and education and really changed my life.

MAILER: Well, I grew up on that: fighting and fucking was what made a good book. But you're doomed if you write about it.

LEEDS: Yeah, but the important thing for me was that things happened in your books, yours and Hemingway's. Obviously you're not the only two authors, but you were the only two for me at the time I started growing up again in literature, and I was so grateful that people didn't just sit around eating cucumber sandwiches and drinking tea. And then I read this in your introduction to *A Transit to Narcissus*. You said, "I do not recognize the young man who wrote this book, I do not even like him very much, and yet I know that he must be me because his themes are mine, his ambition is as large for his age as my ambition would ever become, and I am not even without an odd regard for him. If I understand what he is trying to say, then he is close to saying the unsayable. The most terrible themes of my own life: the nearness of violence to creation, and the whiff of murder just beyond every embrace of love are his themes also." It occurs to me that although you're obviously evolving over these forty-odd years into a different kind of writer all the time, these thematic preoccupations really have remained constant — not static, but constant — and I wonder if you feel that being thus preoccupied has hurt you, in that so many critics have been shortsighted about roundly attacking your work for those reasons.

MAILER: At the least it's made me hard to read for a number of people. They approach my books with anxiety, precisely the anxiety that street people feel when they're walking down the street and expect trouble. Most people who read books are — tend to be, at least — superficially gentle and reflective and civilized. They read books to avoid the street. While books about violence are exotic to such readers, they are also disturbing. And I think mine are doubly disturbing because what I'm saying is: look, I'm not asking you to read about violence so you can have a good read; I'm saying there's a lot of meaning in violence. That it's one aspect of a world-wide violence which appropriates us. You know I've been saying from the beginning, of course, there's individual violence versus the violence of the State. It takes a thousand forms. You could say that the spread of social programs is a very subtle form of violence. The scare right now about AIDS is an example of that. One thing doctors are famous for, over the centuries, is that their statistical forecasts are always off. We're being told now that a world-wide AIDS plague is coming. The statistics, oddly enough, I don't think necessarily bear it out. For one thing, the rate of AIDS in New York has not been doubling every year as they said it would. The rate of increase has been lowering each year; it's still on the increase, but it's been lowering. There's an inability of doctors to think intimately about these problems. I have a theory on AIDS, for what it's worth. The question I raise is which kinds of homosexuals are decimated by AIDS? It seems to me that there are a great many homosexuals who have two practices. They're not only promiscuous in sex, but they're promiscuous in their use of antibiotics. The literature's just filled with cases of people who go to Turkish baths and make love with ten men and then go home and inject themselves with penicillin. I think they should make one simple study which is to try to find out how much in the way of antibiotics AIDS victims have taken in relation to the general population. My guess is that four or five times as much antibiotics has entered their blood streams before they got the AIDS. People have been promiscuous before and after Christ. Why does AIDS strike now? That kind of promiscuity has been going on from the birth of time with certain people, so this plague, I think, is not a reflection of promiscuity, it's a reflection of antibiotics. I would say ultimately (and this sounds mad, but it has to be taken as just an example of the way I think) if you extend your concepts far enough, antibiotics are a form of violence, a very attenuated form of social violence practiced upon people. Nobody ever asks us; nobody ever laid it out for us when it first came along. Doctors just said, "Here, take this. It's good for you. It'll cure your illness." The notion that illness might not be there to be cured by external means but was supposed to be cured from within is a desperately conservative notion. It's never been explored.

LEEDS: Your extra-medical theories are going to have to be way out before I don't take them seriously, because in 1965 in *An American Dream* and in 1966 in *Cannibals and Christians*, when you codified your visions about cancer, I called my brother who was in medical school at the time. I read him the passage about patients firing out of the windows from cancer wards at people in the streets and the possibility of miraculous cures, and I said, "Is this way out?" And he said, "We don't know." And since then, of course, it's become less and less outlandish an idea, as you're well aware; so I take these extra-medical theories you come up with quite seriously. One other thing you said earlier that I wanted to address is that you've always felt that the institutionalized violence of the State is far more horrendous than individual acts of violence. I understand that entirely in terms of Gary Gilmore, but I wonder what you think about the Bernhard Goetz case?

MAILER: Oh, I think like everybody else I'm mired in confusion on that one. First of all, I don't know what really happened there. I'm not sure Goetz knows what happened.

It's one thing to defend yourself; it's another to take advantage of having a gun. And I think the truth there lies somewhere in between, so I've got to waffle on that one. If we could talk about an ideal approach to these matters, I'd say no one should ever have a gun, and everyone should know how to fight.

LEEDS: Right.

MAILER: If everyone knew how to fight, there would certainly be no more fights than there are now, probably fewer. When violent people hang out together they tend to balance each other out. It's even an aesthetic principle. *Prizzi's Honor* proves it; you can find an interesting love story between two killers for hire because they're equal in the same way that two gentle, civilized people are equal. That is, a love story between Virginia Woolf and Leonard Woolf is as interesting as a love story between Jack Nicholson and Kathleen Turner, because they're equals.

LEEDS: This thing about balancing out is true. Sometimes it seems to me that you're never as safe as you are in a bad bar where nobody knows what you know or how fast you are or how bad you are: that everybody pretty much leaves each other alone.

MAILER: Well, they know the price of violence. The most dangerous situation, always, is when you have one person who's violent among a great many people who are not. That's always an unstable situation — that's explosive.

LEEDS: One of the things about your work and you is that I can't get away from it, which is to say that I've obviously read and taught and written on other authors, but I'm always finding your name every place I turn, and I don't just mean in *Newsweek*. I was just reading Philip Roth's latest novel, *The Counterlife*...

MAILER: I heard about that.

LEEDS: Would you like to see this quotation?

MAILER: I never saw the passage.

LEEDS: You can keep this copy if you like. It's really interesting. Zuckerman, Roth's character, the novelist, is in Israel, and the wife of this Meyer Kahane type of political rabbi says, "Let me ask you a question. You are a friend of Norman Mailer?" "Both of us write books." "Let me ask you a question about your colleague Mailer. Why is he so interested in murder and criminals and killing? When I was at Barnard, our English professor assigned those books to read — books by a Jew who cannot stop thinking about murder and criminals and killing. Sometimes when I think back to the innocence of that class and the idiotic nonsense that they said there, I think, why didn't I ask 'If this Jew is so exhilarated by violence, why doesn't he go to Israel?'" [laughter]

MAILER: That's funny.

LEEDS: Of course, on the next page, he defends the nature of the creative experience and such, but I thought you'd get a kick out of that. In line with something else you were saying, in *Fools Die* you probably know that Mario Puzo's got a character called Osano who bears some resemblance to you...

MAILER: Well, very little in a funny way because he smokes cigars which I hate and anyone who knows anything at all about me will know... I can think of three things I don't like. Cigars are probably the first, and the other is he has me killing a poodle. I had a poodle for eighteen years, so I resented that directly. You know, if I were to kill a dog, a poodle would be the last one.

LEEDS: Well, there may be aspects of Puzo himself there, because I think he's a cigar smoker, and maybe he hates poodles. But anyway, Osano is always taking penicillin. That's one of the reasons I brought it up. Every time he has a sexual encounter, which is frequently, he prophylactically takes penicillin which is why, ultimately, he dies of syphilis. But here's the thing that really fascinated me...

MAILER: It's interesting to do that kind of job on a guy. It's something Jackie Susann used to do which is to put you into a book so people say "Oh yes, that's Norman Mailer" and then give you all the things you never do and that's double punishment. Not only are you written about badly, but inaccurately, and people believe it. I'm sorry, you were saying...

LEEDS: Well, the amazing thing is, I was rereading *Fools Die*, and Puzo's got a passage written by Osano, in which he's talking about women. He says, "I have plans for [the woman I love]. I have dark graves in caves to hide her head." I said, Jesus Christ, this was years before *Tough Guys Don't Dance* was written. What an amazing coincidence. Maybe I'm making too much of it.

MAILER: No. That's interesting. I think Puzo's a gambler, and gamblers are incredibly instinctive. They're always either right or wrong. People who tend to be either right or wrong become gamblers. It's a way of searching out that potentiality in oneself. So he obviously hit on a theme. I never read *Fools Die*. Directly of course, you know, the decapitations in *Tough Guys* come out of that case with Tony Costa up in Provincetown where he dismembered four women's bodies. Well, that thing haunted me for years, and you know one reason why, of course, is you're probably familiar with that introduction to *Why Are We in Vietnam?*

LEEDS: Yes, right.

MAILER: I was going to write about a group of people

hiding out in the sand dunes of Provincetown who were making raids and killing and then along came Manson. That freaked me. And then Tony Costa a few years later.

LEEDS: Was there a reason—this is fascinating to me personally—that in *Tough Guys Don't Dance* you returned to writing about a middle-aged character? I know that in *Armies* you said that there were parts of yourself that were nineteen and seventy-three and forty-four, and of course in *Ancient Evenings* Menenhetet is all ages, but it fascinates me, being middle-aged now myself...

MAILER: Listen, you look in great shape.

LEEDS: Thank you. It intrigues me when I go back and look at *An American Dream*, which is really my favorite among the works; I know there are greater books, but it's the one that speaks to me most personally. And I was looking at the preface to *Deaths for the Ladies*, a book which I think I understood too quickly, and then here you went back again to writing about a middle-aged protagonist. Was there a reason that you revisited not only those haunts but that period?

MAILER: Yeah. One thing that literary critics don't pay enough attention to is the practicality of writers' themes. That is, you take a theme that you can handle. I had a set of objective circumstances. I had to write a book in two months and I had been unable to write this novel for a long time. For about a year I'd been trying to start it. I couldn't find my protagonist and I knew I was down to two months. So, I took one who would be comfortable. The only way to do a book quickly, I think, is to write in the first person, but you've got to have someone who's near enough to yourself so that he's comfortable. I chose a man who was not at all me in any real way, but was near enough so that his style wouldn't seem false to me.

In other words, I wouldn't have to stretch for a style. I tried someone who could conceivably have read my work and argued with it, liked one book, not liked another. I would have been one of fifty-eight authors who made up his—what can I say—the dome of his aesthetic purview; and that was crucial. A lot comes out of that. In other words, I took someone who was middle-aged because to write about someone who was young would have been too great a stretch and my own age would have interfered in other ways. I didn't want to write about someone too near to me. Then I'd get involved with myself while writing the book. All these things were determined by the fact that the book had to be written quickly. You know, in movie-making, parenthetically, they have a wonderful phrase: "Do what is necessary." In other words, if you have to get a scene in before dark, the director will say, "Do what is necessary," and what that means is, we'll get the shot in whether it's good or it's bad. We'll have it by dark because otherwise we're lost. *Tough Guys* is an example of what happens when you have to do what is necessary. The book took two months to write. If I'd had more time, it might have taken a year because I would have had time to go off on excursions that I couldn't afford any longer. Once you can only afford the task before you, you work quickly provided you've gotten yourself into a simple frame of mind. Most writing consists of getting into that simple frame of mind; it's very, very hard to do. You know there's so much to write about and you've chosen a little and that's always irksome, and one's always rebelling against how little there is to write about in the particular book you've chosen.

LEEDS: Speaking of the movie version, after doing those three movies in the late '60s that were so relatively unstructured, was it an interesting challenge, and were there any particular problems working from a structured script?

MAILER: It was altogether different. It was as different as boxing and wrestling. The movies I made all those years ago were great fun, wonderful fun. Making *Maidstone* was probably the most interesting week of my life. But now I had a budget, an expensive budget for me—small for a mainstream film—but still it was five million dollars. I had a schedule to keep to. I had movie stars; I had a script, a most detailed script. So it was different. I had to function with that. I wouldn't have dreamed of improvising much.

LEEDS: Did you enjoy it?

MAILER: Oh, I enjoyed it a lot. The trouble is, I like making movies more than writing now. I'm tired of writing. I've been doing it for forty years, and there's not much fun left. I get a hold of myself in the morning and go into that room and dig more stuff out of the old gut. The gut rebels. It's tired of being called on to perform these yeoman duties. Whereas in making a movie you're really not an artist, more an aesthetic engineer. You've got a lot of talented people working under you and they come up to you and you've got to make instantaneous decisions about matters you know very little about. Like hairdo, costume. And so it's kind of fun. You're using everything you've ever learned to the best of your ability. It kept reminding me about being at war but in a good way. It was like the ideal war. Nobody got killed, but you ate in a different place every day, usually standing up. There were vehicles. The biggest problem, just as it was in the army, was where do you put the vehicles. You know when you pick a location shot, you pick it by its availability to a road. You could be in the deepest forest you ever saw, but it's got to be 100 yards from the road because that's where the trucks are parked. So there's a reverse logic in filmmaking. You start with the costs and work toward the art.

LEEDS: Did you enjoy working with Ryan O'Neal?

MAILER: Oh, well, that was heaven in a crazy way. Heaven is the wrong word. Ryan is a very, very bright guy. Word for word, sentence for sentence, he's smarter than I am. He's very quick. He's that way as a boxer. He's a very fast boxer and you can't win exchanges with him. He's terribly funny on the set. He's very generous. And the reason he's difficult is he's too generous, so he gives and gives and gives of himself and then at a certain point he's given too much. Then he gets into a black Irish mood and woe to the first person who crosses him at that point.

LEEDS: He sounds like Tim Madden.

MAILER: No, he's different from Tim Madden, but I think he's done an incredible performance in the film. I think maybe it's the best thing he's ever done.

LEEDS: When's it going to be out?

MAILER: October, if everything holds together.

LEEDS: I loved your interview with Clint Eastwood in *Parade* a few years ago. I'm a big Clint Eastwood fan and I agree with you that *Honky Tonk Man* is his best film. But do you get the idea as I do that he's really a bright guy who... Here's my theory: that he got really mad at the American public when *Honky Tonk Man* didn't go well; it's such a sensitive film. So in the next one, *Sudden Impact*, he gets the .44 Magnum automatic that takes a shell the size of a beer can and blows up buildings. It seemed to me that this was intentional self-parody, that he said, "You want Dirty Harry, you're gonna get Dirty Harry."

MAILER: Well, I think so. You know it's very hard to understand the psychology of these big stars. Take guys like Burt Reynolds and Clint Eastwood and Stallone. I think they're enormously competitive people or they wouldn't be where they are. I think they see themselves as champs in what they do. And they hate losing. They hate losing the way a heavyweight champion hates losing a fight, and so if they make a movie and it doesn't do well at the box office, they can't get it out of their systems. It eats at them. It terrifies them. It terrifies them the way a heavyweight champion is terrified if he loses a fight, or even if a sparring partner makes him look bad on a given day. Their ego has the same...I once made the remark that heavyweight champions always verge on the edge of being insane. Because conceivably they were the toughest guys in the world and conceivably they weren't. There could always be some guy waiting for them in an alley, some maniac who one way or another could take them in a street fight. They just didn't know. They couldn't know if they were the toughest guy around or weren't and this has to eat at a man's stability. In the same way, movie stars have to feel: what are they made of, what are their ingredients? I'd hate to be a movie star on a bad day, waking up with a hangover and a dull fight with one's woman and feeling unattractive. That's a tough combination to contend with. I guess that's one reason they're so health conscious. The few I've known take enormous care of themselves, eat very properly. Eastwood's that way. He really watches his diet. Warren Beatty's that way. Beatty, who's a sensitive and very intelligent man, is a little off to the side. He won't put himself in the movies the way the others do. I mean, I think Burt Reynolds is just full of rage if a film doesn't score. You know, one of my favorite teasing notions — I'm absolutely serious about it, but no one will ever believe it — is (I would hope by '88 or '92; it probably won't be until 1996) that the best presidential contest we could have would be between Warren Beatty for the Democrats and Clint Eastwood for the Republicans.

LEEDS: This is a question I've wanted to ask you since 1983. Do you still have the same master plan for the *Ancient Evenings* trilogy?

MAILER: No. And the reason I gave it up is the second book was going to be science fiction. And I just came to a sobering estimate of my ability to retain difficult material. First of all, I don't think the economics will ever come together because I'd need a year of serious reading to catch up on all the scientific material because if I were going to do a book on science fiction I'd want to do it so I'd become a sort of master of the medium, and that would take an awful lot of thinking, and I don't think well scientifically. I can tell because I've subscribed to *Scientific American* for fifteen years now, and I find more and more difficulty keeping up with the articles, which is a measure of your ability to understand those concepts. The concepts of science are getting more and more difficult for me all the time so I thought, what's the sense of writing such a book? I can't if I'm going to end up faking it.

LEEDS: It really surprises me that you say that about yourself and science because I thought that in *Of a Fire on the Moon* your training in aeronautical engineering obviously shows through.

MAILER: It was a help. No, that was not a bad book, and I think that if I was going to write a trilogy which was already in my mind then, I think in a funny way I blew it by writing *Of a Fire on the Moon*. I was very depressed the entire time I was writing that book, and usually, when you're very depressed writing a book it's because you're not writing the book you should have been writing. You're using up something that should have gone into another book, and I think that's exactly what I got into there. The excitement I felt about writing about science went into that book, and there was very little left over to do the science fiction book and I've been dawdling on it. So that's one reason why I don't think the trilogy will ever be fulfilled, and the other is that I've lost the feeling that it counts. I think there are very few people anymore who really care whether you do a trilogy like that. So you'd be the weekend sensation in *The New York Times Book Review* and then that'd be it. No one would ever read it. One of the things that startled me was how few people ever made any attempt to read *Ancient Evenings*. Even people who love my work just said, "Well, gee, I couldn't get into it," so...

LEEDS: It drives me crazy when I hear that.

MAILER: Well, I do think there's a crisis in literature that's profound. It eats at everyone, including me. I've lost some of my sense of high purpose and I think readers of literature have also lost it. TV is the true AIDS of our time. There's no mental immunology left for culture. Culture is totally infected by TV.

LEEDS: One of my students came up to me—I always assign *The Naked and the Dead* the first week of classes. I get a lot of dropouts because of that, but the ones that stick with it love it. And this young girl (remember when we used to be able to call them girls?) came up to me...

MAILER: What do you have to say? This *person* came up?

LEEDS: Well, woman, even if they're thirteen. Of course, my students are all over eighteen. I think that the eighteen-year-old girls today are not militant about that; they don't care if you call them girls anymore. I think it's the people who came up during the movement that still take that seriously. But, anyway, this young woman came up to me—she's holding the Rinehart edition that you need a wheelbarrow to bring to class—and she said, "Is there a video on this?" [laughter] I love that.

MAILER: Is it that they read *The Naked and the Dead* and they drop out, why? Too long a book?

LEEDS: No, they *don't* read it and they drop out. They see how big it is, and they say, "Have I got to read this? Wow!" And I say to them, "If you don't like reading and talking about books and writing about them, then drop out." So a lot of them drop out and the ones I keep are great kids and they usually love the book. After forty years... Here's a quotation that's always intrigued me out of *An American Dream*: "No, men were afraid of murder, but not from a terror of justice so much as the knowledge that a killer attracted the attention of the gods; then your mind was not your own, your anxiety ceased to be neurotic, your dread was real. Omens were as tangible as bread. There was an architecture to eternity"—That's the line that rings for me. I wanted that to be the full title of my first book about you: *An Architecture to Eternity: The Structured Vision of Norman Mailer*—"There was an architecture to eternity which housed us as we dreamed, and when there was murder, a cry went through the market places of sleep. Eternity had been deprived of a room. Somewhere the divine rage met a fury." This sense of the cosmic order and an embattled God is something that obviously has pervaded your work, but do you feel that in recent years it's been expanded, refined, changed in any way?

MAILER: I think it has. You know if I end up writing a few more good books then those refinements ideally will find their way into that. I still would subscribe to every single thing that's said there. That hasn't changed a bit. Henry Kissinger once said to me, "I haven't had a new idea since I've been in government. You see, I'm working with all old ideas." And he's a very bright man, obviously, a man who prides himself in his ability to think and to have new thoughts. That's the joy of life to many people and certainly to him, and I feel that way. But I find that idea you've just quoted is the key of all my ideas. There are little variations on it all the time, but to attempt to talk to you about it now, how it's changed, all I can say is it hasn't really changed that much. I'm still trying to find a way to embody all that in a book where it truly works for a reader who's never encountered these notions before.

LEEDS: Yeah — who hasn't been a charter subscriber all along.

MAILER: Another reason why I was so drawn to writing about Gary Gilmore is I had the feeling deep down he believed the same thing. I found him a funny man and parts of him I understand perfectly; other parts of him to this day I don't have a clue. He had a quirky dull streak that I've never gotten near, but the side of him that wanted to die I understand perfectly. It was almost like he was dramatizing one of my favorite notions, that the soul can die before the body, and was quite aware of that and was determined not to let that happen and in that sense was heroic.

LEEDS: I understand that. Speaking of criminals and of cops, too, I'd like to talk to you about Dougy "Big Mac"

Madden [in *Tough Guys Don't Dance*]. One thing about Dougy is that he looks like a detective but he hates cops, and I think that a lot of people have been attracted or repelled by your interest in the criminal mentality, but they forget that you deal almost as much with the psychology of cops. You played a criminal in *Wild 90*, but a cop, a lieutenant, in *Beyond the Law*, and obviously it's the other side of the same coin. Do you know a lot of cops? My dad was a cop for twenty-one years in New York City and we had cops around the house all the time.

MAILER: I have a friend who's a detective on the police force and he gave me this.

LEEDS: It's a miniature detective shield.

MAILER: Yeah. I'm fascinated with cops. I love good cops. I really think that it's such an extraordinary thing to be a good cop, it's so difficult, and a good cop probably has more temptations than any man in any profession you could name. And to keep their balance in the middle of all those conflicting forces...so I have two fondnesses. One's for a good cop; the other's for a good crook.

LEEDS: I knew the latter but I didn't know if I should mention cops because for the most part in the books and even in the nonfiction, you're pretty negative about them. But I have to come clean, that while my dad probably would share a lot of the same views — he's in his seventies now — that you have about crooked cops, there were cops around in my life as I was growing up and in fact I used to impersonate one when we went to police conventions after I got big enough to look like I might be a young cop.

MAILER: Casting would always put you in as a cop.

LEEDS: Thanks, I hope that's positive. Anyway, the thing is, those guys are really fun to be around. They're crazy in a weird way. All those Wambaugh novels...

MAILER: They have the most powerful dirty minds. A sense of motive...so mean and strong. I think it would be a marvelous novel to write about a good cop, but the only reason I've never been drawn toward it is because it's been so abused. I mean you can't turn on the television without finding a good cop. I'm so sick of that theme. I think it's been so abused. It's always used for ulterior motives. The worst forces of law and order are always used in the portrait of the good cop so I tend not to get into that, not much. But it would make a marvelous novel if you could find a way to do it.

LEEDS: I started talking about Dougy. The thing about Dougy that fascinates me is that there's very little about fathers in your earlier works. Mikey Lovett is an amnesiac and Sergius' father throws him into an orphanage, and then suddenly here's this very positive, massive father figure. Could I ask...

MAILER: Nothing to do with my father. My father was a small...a smaller man.

LEEDS: I didn't assume that...

MAILER: You mean, why? Why did I get into it? I think it's the sort of thing you get into when you get into it. I've never written about childhood. I don't want to until the day I can really write about childhood. I don't want to write about anything unless I can do something with it that hasn't quite been done before. So that's all I ever ask of a book is that I have something new to say. I don't really want to write the same book other people are writing and so I've never found that moment when I could write about childhood. I may before I'm done. I've never really written about a father and a son until *Tough Guys*. I think it's the best thing in the book probably.

LEEDS: There are some touching scenes there.

MAILER: In the movie it gets lost to a degree because there's no room for it. You know who played Dougy Madden? Larry Tierney. Remember who did *Dillinger*? I think people are going to like him a lot.

LEEDS: I'm really looking forward to that movie. By the way, are the three earlier movies available on cassettes?

MAILER: No, it's too expensive. It would cost seven hundred bucks to make one of them into a cassette, but I can't afford it.

LEEDS: You know, there'd be a market. This pal of mine teaches a movie course, and he got *Wild 90* and I came in and gave a guest lecture. And then he got *Beyond the Law*, and then we couldn't get *Maidstone* and they said at the rental place that you had the only copy. Apparently you had taken it out of circulation.

MAILER: I might have taken it back at a certain point because what had happened was there are very few left and there was no income from them and I just thought they'd get chewed up, there would be nothing left at all, so I took them out of circulation.

LEEDS: You were talking about dogs earlier and I'm struck by "Stunts" in *Tough Guys*. When you mentioned owning a poodle for eighteen years, was that by any chance the dog you got in a fight about with a sailor in a bar because he called your dog a fag?

MAILER: Yeah. It was on the street actually. I had two dogs at the time. At that point Tibo had a wife who we later gave away because we came back from the country with Tibo and the wife and a pup and walking three dogs on a New York street got to be hilarious. I couldn't handle it. With three leashes.

So we gave away two of them.

LEEDS: That's a scene worthy of Charlie Chaplin. And I also like the story about Karl the German shepherd and Dorothy Parker's dog…I was thinking about other writers. I'm certainly not going to get into the Farrell, Dos Passos, Steinbeck things that people ask you about all the time, but I just have to tell you that in terms of Hemingway, I keep finding you saying new things about him that always warm me because he's been so central to my life. I thought that in *Advertisements*, first of all, that capsule criticism of *The Old Man and the Sea* said more about that book than many long essays did. But I really was pleased that you said in a recent interview, "After *Executioner's Song* I realized how very talented he was." I found that very heartwarming. I thought it was a very gracious thing to say.

MAILER: Well, he is, he was. Did you read that attack on Scribner's in *The New Republic* by Barbara Probst Solomon? Look for it in the library. Barbara Probst Solomon is a good writer who went and read the original Hemingway manuscript which is over at the Kennedy Library. And she says it's a great miscarriage of literary justice. *The Garden of Eden* as published is a total misrepresentation of the work that Hemingway was doing. The people in the book pass through many years; they're not just young. The thing's totally distorted.

LEEDS: Well, I gather from what Baker said in his biography, purportedly it was in horrendous shape. But I wouldn't presume to know.

MAILER: What she said was that it wasn't in bad shape, that the work would have been more interesting printed the way it was, sprawling all over the place with all the false starts but that finally what we would have seen is half the body of a giant book and that this thing is not Hemingway, that it's been so altered...

LEEDS: It would be more interesting to guys like me. That's sad to hear. Another guy with large ambitions and big books is James Jones, who I know was a friend of yours. And I've always admired that trilogy (or tetralogy if you count *The Pistol*). People used to ask me, "Is *The Naked and the Dead* the great novel of WW II?" and I said, "Sure," and then eventually I had to say, "Maybe not, if you take Jones's books as one massive work."

MAILER: I always thought *Eternity* was a bigger book.

LEEDS: Not just *Eternity* itself, but *Eternity* and *The Pistol* and *The Thin Red Line* and *Whistle* put together, because in a sense he made World War II his Yoknapatawpha County; and I wonder if you feel, because you don't want to keep writing essentially the same book about the same things, that this return to the same central setting and preoccupations is artistically stultifying? Do you think that it shows too much limitation on the part of a writer like Jones?

MAILER: To begin with, a novelist writes the books that he or she can write and this is more true of serious novelists than commercial novelists. But a novelist does the kind of book that they can do until it gets distorted by their ambitions and by their idea of the kind of book to make them immortal. If you're reasonably young when you arrive and start taking yourself seriously long before you've developed your metier then you tend to be very self-conscious. Jones was self-conscious. Styron and I are, to a degree, even to this day still a bit self-conscious because very early in life we were handed a role. We were young major novelists and it's a terribly funny role. You have to live up to it. You tend to think that way. I think Jones probably wrestled with the idea: Is this good or bad for my career to do a tetralogy on the war? He may have lost energy in thinking about it too much. I've tried to avoid those traps. I may have set myself a trap with the three big books, you see, and spent an awful lot of time thinking: Will I do it, should I do it, is it worth doing, can I do it? All those questions. And finally, writing novels at this point in my life is a little bit like falling in love: it isn't automatic. You know, one may never fall in love again with someone new and one may never get another novel, or one may; one may get five novels. You just don't know. You don't know if you're going to have a thrill-filled old age with five novels yet to be written or whether you'll dry up slowly and fall off the tree.

LEEDS: I know which way I'm betting.

MAILER: Well, I was struck when I started making this movie about how much I was enjoying it, compared to the way I felt about writing for the last fifteen years. Something had gone out of the writing, maybe the belief that it makes a difference. I can't tell you what that does to effort. How vitiating to feel it just doesn't matter that much.

LEEDS: Fitzgerald said something very similar when movies were in their infancy, and Kesey said something very similar last fall at Town Hall. He said, "If Chekhov were alive today, he'd be using a video recorder," and he said that's why the Alaskan novel [*Sailor Song*] or whatever the next one may eventually be isn't getting written. But Kesey showed so much promise. I don't know if you ever read *Sometimes a Great Notion*, but it's about fifty times greater than *Cuckoo's Nest*.

MAILER: Really.

LEEDS: Yeah. It's a wonderful novel and I wonder if you're willing to say something about the kind of novelist who only tells us one or two stories and then stops. I guess we're lucky to get what we do but we don't get any more.

MAILER: Kesey certainly has an enormous amount to write about. Writers who write just a few books…I think nobody knows how much damage a book does to you except another writer. It's hell writing a novel; you really poison your body doing it. It's an unnatural physical activity to sit at a desk and squeeze words out of yourself. It means that you secrete various kinds of fatigues and poisons through your system that you don't get rid of easily. As you get older, it's worse. The other reason why I've been so obsessed with prize fighters is the idea of the aging prize fighter who has to get into shape for one more fight and knows the damage that fight is going to do to his body, which is already beginning to worsen; it puts him in a gloom. One of the things that characterizes almost every older fighter I've ever seen training for a fight is the depression that hangs over him and his camp because the only thing good that can come out of it is money. The rest is all a foregone conclusion. Even if he wins the fight — even if he wins it well — he's not going to get a new purchase on life out of the fight the way a young fighter can by a decisive victory. And that's true in writing. Writers will often make grave decisions — am I going to write this book or not? And at a certain point you have to believe that the book can be enormously important or you won't suffer that kind of self-destruction. Because it is self-destruction, it's quiet self-destruction, civilized self-destruction. Let's say in writing a novel over two or three years of the hardest work, that the damage it does to the body is equal to someone who has never smoked before taking on two or three packs a day for a few years. And I think if you could weigh those things you'd find it's accurate. I think one reason I've always been such an amateur about medicine and so interested in it at a great remove is because when you're a writer, in a certain sense you're a doctor to yourself. You're always feeling these various tensions and ailments creep into you. From an early age writers become hypochondriacs. It goes with the territory. Your factory is yourself. You're always examining the factory for potential breakdowns, anticipating troubles, and so you get to be awfully alert to the relation not only between yourself and the world but the relationship between yourself and your body. And writing impinges on your body.

LEEDS: One of my favorite quotations about you is the opening of Joan Didion's review in *The New York Times Book Review* of *The Executioner's Song*, where she said so many people read you only within their own limitations. I just wanted to ask you, do you like her work?

MAILER: I have a lot of respect for her work. I once said that if there were a particular woman writer today in America whom you could compare to Hemingway, it'd probably be Joan Didion.

LEEDS: Absolutely.

MAILER: She has that same sense of the power of the sentence sitting by itself and the power of the next sentence. There's no accident that she writes movies and lives with film because her work, like Hemingway's, is montage. That is, there's an assumption that the reader's going to pay enough attention to each sentence so they'll feel the next sentence come into place. It's very much like cuts in a film. Sentences don't have to exist entirely by themselves; they exist by their relation to the next sentence and the echo of the sentence that just passed. She writes marvelous prose. Another thing about Hemingway that I liked so much after I finished *The Executioner's Song* is…I was doing that a little bit in *The Executioner's Song* but it just didn't compare. Pick up Hemingway and read him, and boy, you feel that montage. People who write in a simple style, like Raymond Carver, depend on montage. You can't write in a simple style and get away with it unless you can do that... Those choices have to be exquisite—what goes next to what.

LEEDS: I wanted to ask you about a guy I'm interested in, Harry Crews, whom you mention in *Tough Guys Don't Dance*. Spider Nissen and Tim are always going through this list of writers and he's one of the guys they rip up once in a while. But here's a quotation that I like from an essay he wrote. He says, "I'm sick and tired of women in my face and on my case and I'm sick and tired of being sick and tired." [laughter] I thought that's something that might interest you. I know you gave him a blurb for *A Feast of Snakes*.

MAILER: Yeah. I think he's very funny and very tough and kind of incorruptible. Like he's set his course and if storms come across, then they come, it's all right, but he's staying on that course. He knows what he knows and he's going to write about it. He has a clarity of purpose in his writing that I like.

LEEDS: Yeah, you can see it in his face.

MAILER: I've never met him.

LEEDS: No, I haven't met him but on every book jacket his face gets fiercer; he's got lines on lines and this forceful scowl and you can just see that he's an uncompromising guy.

[Perhaps fifteen minutes of informal chat and amenities ensues.]

LEEDS: Thanks for inviting me, Norman, and good luck on the movie.

MAILER: Thank you, Barry.

CHAPTER 8

THE CRITICAL CLIMATE: BOOKS ON MAILER

Since 1969, when *The Structured Vision of Norman Mailer* was published, there has been a flood (and possibly a slight ebb recently) of works on Mailer. These include critical studies, biographies and collections of essays.

As early as 1968, Richard Foster had written a fine monograph entitled *Norman Mailer* for the *University of Minnesota Pamphlets on American Authors* series. Foster evinces a sophisticated understanding of Mailer's work through *The Armies of the Night*, and presents it clearly in a style that combines brevity with depth.

Donald L. Kaufmann's *Norman Mailer: The Countdown (The First Twenty Years)* (1969) stops treating Mailer's work at 1966 and employs a strange structure that begins with Chapter 10 and "counts down" to Chapter 1, moving "from literature as such, to literature as public statement, and finally, to literature as private vision" (xvi). Kaufmann concludes his

Chapter 7, "The time seems ripe for Mailer's goodbye to politics…," a pronouncement which had already been proven false by the publication of *The Armies of the Night* and *Miami and the Siege of Chicago*, to say nothing of the political writings to come.

In 1970, Joe Flaherty published *Managing Mailer*, an account of his experiences as campaign manager for Mailer and Jimmy Breslin in their mayoral campaign of 1969.

Robert F. Lucid's collection of critical essays, *Norman Mailer: The Man and his Work* (1971), was the first of five such collections to date. Most of the seventeen pieces included were by such major critics as Diana Trilling, Norman Podhoretz and John W. Aldridge, or novelists like Gore Vidal, Tom Wolfe and James Baldwin, and although many of these had been reprinted elsewhere, some of them several times, it was useful to have them readily accessible in one book. Lucid also performed the useful and intelligent service of reprinting Foster's *Norman Mailer*, and even concluded by reprinting a *Playboy* interview with Mailer. He also included a pioneering checklist of Mailer's work, the basis for later bibliographies.

Leo Braudy's collection, *Twentieth Century Views of Norman Mailer* (1972), is similar to, though shorter than, Lucid's collection. Both comprise useful and intelligent essays by major critics. Braudy's book contains thirteen essays (compared to Lucid's eighteen) of which three (by Diana Trilling, James Baldwin and Leo Bersani) appear in both books. Three critics (Aldridge, Foster and Richard Poirier) are represented in both volumes by different articles. Thus, the two are similar in content, with Lucid enjoying the advantage of greater scope.

Richard Poirier's *Norman Mailer* (1972) in the Viking *Modern Masters* series was the best book on Mailer at the time of its publication, and may still be. This intelligent assessment of the author's career by a critic of established reputation is precise and original in perception and quite sophisticated in its style and argument, especially on Mailer's rhetoric.

In 1974, Robert Solotaroff published *Down Mailer's Way*. During this period of new books on Mailer appearing in close succession, Solotaroff was a step ahead of Poirier in discussing *St. George and the Godfather* and already a step behind Mailer in omitting *Marilyn*. Solotaroff is forceful in his views, even when he admits that they have changed (he grants that his evaluation of *An American Dream*, for example, had been too simplistic at first), and he tends to rather procrustean interpretations, a criticism which he anticipates but does not necessarily disarm effectively. His critique of "The White Negro" is one of the most penetrating.

Also issued in 1974 was Laura Adams's *Will the Real Norman Mailer Please Stand Up*, a useful collection of essays in which Mailer is presented in his various roles, such as novelist, poet, playwright, filmmaker, journalist and politician, with several overviews as well. The essays include some by such major writers as Joyce Carol Oates, Tony Tanner and Richard Poirier. In the same year, Adams also published *Norman Mailer: A Comprehensive Bibliography*.

Jean Radford, in *Norman Mailer: A Critical Study* (1975), did not fully utilize the opportunity to deal with Mailer's most recent work at the time. She focuses on works published by 1968, treats those through 1971 with relative brevity, and adds an epilogue on *St. George, Existential Errands*, and *Marilyn*. This competent work offers recapitulations of points made by earlier critics, enlivened by some new perceptions, notably a discussion of Mailer's problems with fictional voice. Late in the book, Radford's hitherto measured criticism gives way to reiterations of the doctrinaire charge of sexism in Mailer's work and the fashionable Mailer-baiting popularized by Kate Millett in *Sexual Politics* (1970).

Stanley T. Gutman's *Mankind in Barbary: The Individual and Society in the Novels of Norman Mailer* (1975) is limited primarily to Mailer's five novels to date, plus "The White Negro" and *The Armies of the Night*, with a brief epilogue touching on several of Mailer's more recent works. He concludes that the promise shown in *Armies* has not yet been realized, but that on the evidence of *Marilyn*, Mailer "may yet…become the outstanding novelist of our age" (203).

Laura Adams published her own full-length critical study, *Existential Battles: The Growth of Norman Mailer,* in 1976. This perceptive work deals, as its title suggests, with Mailer's personal and artistic growth through his existential vision. The conclusion of Adams's book is forceful:

> Of course, he has been laying his big novel before us all along: its subject matter the territory he has regained from the totalitarians for the humanists, and its style the creation of himself. In time we will learn his value to us, if we become existentialists too (180).

In 1977, Frank D. McConnell produced a book entitled *Four Postwar American Novelists: Bellow, Mailer, Barth and Pynchon*. Aimed at a highly sophisticated reading audience, this intelligent work is stylistically complex, often arcane in its analogies, sometimes insistently rigid in its interpretations, but definitely worthy of careful reading. Devoting one long chapter to each of these authors, McConnell deals with their major fiction to date, treating each novel separately, in chronological order. McConnell commits an occasional oversimplification or error of fact. For example, in his passage on *An American Dream*, he bases his comparison of the novel to Alfred Hitchcock's 1960 film *Psycho* partially on the "fact" that Janet Leigh, disposed of early in the Hitchcock movie, suffers a similar fate as Deborah in the movie version of *Dream*. Actually, Eleanor Parker played Deborah while Janet Leigh played Cherry, who survives in the movie. Nonetheless, McConnell moves with impressive brevity from necessary plot summary to intelligent exegesis to an incisive overview of the individual novelist's art and its place in the American literary continuum. More than a series of essays, the book is a cohesive, carefully structured whole, drawing upon particulars to abstract a judgment and a celebration of the development of the American novel since World War II.

Philip Bufithis published a concise and intelligent book, *Norman Mailer*, in 1978 which is consistent with the accessibility and high quality of the Ungar *Modern Literature Series* in which it appeared. This is an incisive study, precise and effective in style, which recapitulates many points of earlier critics, goes beyond them to present some excellent new perceptions (e.g., regarding Mailer's insights on Henry Miller), and thus provides yet another good introduction to Mailer's career.

In the same year, Robert Ehrlich's *Norman Mailer: The Radical as Hipster* was published. Despite some questionable interpretations (Kelly is seen as successfully resisting his incestuous impulse towards Deborah [82]; the artistic success of *An American Dream* is minimized [174]; journalism is viewed as "Mailer's most significant achievement" [174]), Ehrlich presents an intelligent and well-written overview of Mailer's works, dealing in depth with those through 1983.

The third of the critical studies appearing in 1978, Robert Merrill's *Norman Mailer* in the *Twayne's United States Authors Series* presents the assertion that "... nowhere exists the full-length aesthetic evaluation [of Mailer's work].... My book is intended to fill this gap" (12). His most startling and questionable critical judgement is the dismissal of *An American Dream* and *Why Are We in Vietnam?* as "formal failures [which] incorporate several fictional strategies without achieving the unity of any single strategy" (67). In his second edition, *Norman Mailer Revisited* (1992), Merrill courageously maintains this conviction:

> I fear that Chapter 4 (on *An American Dream*
> and *Why Are We in Vietnam?*[1967]) is the least
> revised of my older chapters. Even friendly re-
> viewers of the first edition questioned my lack
> of enthusiasm for the novels of the 1960s, but I
> find that my views are substantially unchanged.
> Solotaroff and I seem to be the only Mailerians
> who do not share Mailer's view that *An Ameri-
> can Dream* is "perhaps my best book" (xiv).

In keeping with the purpose of the series, Merrill's study provides a good introduction to Mailer for the intelligent reader, and covers more territory than most critics.

Sandy Cohen's monograph, *Norman Mailer's Novels* (1979), adds virtually nothing to the existing scholarship. Cohen's work is incomplete in its treatment of both primary and secondary material, and was outdated before it was published. The short bibliography does not include any criticism after 1972 or any Mailer work since 1973. Cohen presents hurried treatments of the first five novels, plus *The Armies of the Night* and *Marilyn*, which are simplistic, often critically untenable, sometimes factually wrong. For example, Mailer is described as writing for *The Village Voice* between 1948 and 1951, but it was not founded until 1955; and the Shago Martin confrontation in *An American Dream* is entirely omitted. Further, Cohen's work is stylistically awkward, and plagued by numerous errors of mechanics and usage.

In 1980, Robert J. Begiebing made his first, striking foray into Mailer criticism with *Acts of Regeneration: Allegory and Archetype in the Works of Norman Mailer*. Interestingly, Begiebing omits *The Naked and the Dead* because he believes that, unlike the works which follow, it does not employ "true (or archetypal) allegory" (8). Begiebing is most impressive in the first five of his eight chapters, treating the novels through *Vietnam* incisively, with an original perspective and a highly sophisticated style and critical apparatus. His discussion of *Dream* is particularly convincing, demonstrating the intellectual force which would inform his later work on *Ancient Evenings* (see below).

Also published in 1980 was Andrew Gordon's *An American Dreamer: A Psychoanalytic Study of the Fiction of Norman Mailer*. An example of Gordon's Freudian approach is this reading of *Dream*:

> Mailer wanted to return America to an awareness of its suppressed desires, to tap into the buried dream life of the nation...Thus he wrote a novel, *An American Dream* (1965), a

blend of pop fiction thriller and heroic myth. *An American Dream* is a phantasmagoria of the unconscious in which rationality is thrown out the window (along with the hero's wife). In this novel, what Freud called "the primary process," the workings of the id, rules: the dense imagery and symbols seem formed through the psychic processes of condensation and displacement, and the plot is deliberately riddled with bizarre coincidences and irrational and magical events—all the logic of a dream (14).

I find this interpretation and Gordon's psychoanalytic method interesting, but would go beyond the limits he sets, and suggest that *Dream* functions credibly on a literal level as well.

The first full-length biography of Mailer was published in 1982. *Mailer: A Biography* by Hilary Mills grew out of an interview with Mailer for the *Saturday Review*, but was "unauthorized." She interviewed over one hundred principal figures in Mailer's life (including the only interview with his first wife, Beatrice, in any biography), then integrated their statements with excerpts from and summaries of Mailer's works. The result is a happy combination of scholarship and documented gossip that is both intelligent and accessible while almost entirely avoiding the temptation to titillate. A notable exception is Mills' somewhat garish first chapter, which opens with Mailer's appearance at the murder trial of Jack Henry Abbott. In addition, she is occasionally guilty of such simplistic judgments as "Mailer the Messiah would try to outdo Hemingway the Hero" (205). The remainder of the book, however, more than redeems these minor weaknesses. In her carefully balanced treatment of Mailer as man and artist, and her ultimate revelation of his artistic professionalism and bedrock integrity, Mills rises above the *People* magazine mentality of some celebrity biographers to remind us of the strengths of Carlos Baker's now-classic *Ernest Hemingway: A Life Story.*

The second unauthorized biography, Peter Manso's lengthy *Mailer, His Life and Times,* appeared in 1985. It is quite different in format from Mills' book in that editor Manso uses the Studs Terkel device of transcribing the reminiscences of Mailer's wives, relatives, friends, acquaintances and rivals. These have been edited and organized chronologically, so that the book moves from Mailer's birth to Brooklyn childhood to Harvard, through his infantry service in the Pacific, up to 1984. Manso's book is thus somewhat more amorphous, lacking the admittedly subjective shaping views of the earlier biographer, including her comments on Mailer's work, but he did interview over 150 individuals. Manso includes photographs, as does Mills, and a genealogical chart.

J. Michael Lennon's *Critical Essays on Norman Mailer,* published in 1986, is an extremely useful addition to the Mailerian's tools. Most of the pieces included are by recognized critics, and although many have been previously published (such as Joan Didion's forceful review of *The Executioner's Song*), they have not hitherto been readily accessible in one place. Two essays, by Robert F. Lucid and Michael Cowan, were written specifically for inclusion in this volume. The scope of the contents is wide, and is impressively enhanced by Lennon's fine introduction, which exhaustively and intelligently summarizes the enormous mass of primary and secondary material published during the first four decades of Mailer's career.

Mailer's America, by Joseph Wenke (1987), is an intelligent critical study which, as its title suggests, posits the thesis that "Mailer's…continuing attempt to define the meaning of America…has always been his central purpose as a writer" (5). In this well-written book, Wenke draws nice distinctions about the work of previous critics, presents a perceptive and cohesive view of Mailer's body of work, focuses on his identity as a peculiarly American writer and upon his existential vision, and refuses to deal with what he considers the overemphasis on Mailer's personality and public image.

In 1988, Michael Lennon edited *Conversations with Norman Mailer*, a fine collection of thirty-four interviews with Mailer (of more than 500 that he has given) dated from 1948 to 1987, conducted by interviewers such as Lillian Ross, Steven Marcus, George Plimpton, William F. Buckley, Jr., John W. Aldridge, Roger Ebert, Mailer himself, and several of the critics discussed in this chapter (Lucid, Adams, Begiebing). In his introduction, Lennon points out that "Mailer professes to dislike the form, although his distaste is not conspicuous when he is in conversation. Only before or after, when he is considering the form in the abstract, does he deride it. When he is talking…he is all gusto" (xiii).

Robert J. Begiebing returned to Mailer criticism in 1989 with a book which surpassed his *Acts of Regeneration*. In *Toward a New Synthesis: John Fowles, John Gardner, Norman Mailer*, he succeeds in his aim to outline a new synthesis of the "hermetic position [which] tends to view the novel as a closed system or word game… [and] the secular position [which] tends to view the novel as a moral force in the world" (1). Dealing with John Fowles' *The Magus*, John Gardner's *The Sunlight Dialogues,* and most impressively with Mailer's *Ancient Eve-*

nings, Begiebing manifests a comprehensive command of the various critical positions in the current, often vitriolic, academic debate between the application of poststructuralism and more traditional literary criticism. His introduction provides a useful and pithy summary of the primary theories in contention in academe today. Through his own eminently sane reading of these prototypical works by three highly significant novelists, he renders both the novels themselves and literary theory more accessible and intellectually provocative to the reader willing to follow him toward the "new synthesis" he posits.

In *Radical Fictions and the Novels of Norman Mailer* (1990), Nigel Leigh presents a highly cerebral treatment of Mailer's radicalism as expressed in his novels and some of his nonfiction writings. Effectively collating a large mass of primary and critical material, in a text somewhat marred by many mechanical errors, Leigh traces Mailer's obsession with the workings of power in society throughout his personal and artistic development. An example of Leigh's perceptive analysis (as quoted in my Chapter 2, above) is his conviction that "The White Negro" marked the fusion of Freud with Marx in Mailer's work and sparked the consequent shift in his perception of the individual's relation to society.

Richard Godden's *Fictions of Capital: The American Novel from James to Mailer* (1990) is an intelligent if sometimes recondite study which traces the American consumer economy through the works of James, Fitzgerald and Mailer, with excursions into Hemingway and several southern writers, notably Faulkner. As its title suggests, the book is as much a sociological and historical study of consumer capitalism and its effect on economic and social relations as it is a work of literary criticism. Godden's book is marked by a number of fine perceptions about the authors he discusses, including an interesting treatment of the influences of

Fitzgerald upon Mailer.

Carl Rollyson's *The Lives of Norman Mailer: A Biography* (1991) is an accessible critical biography, again unauthorized, which seems of more use to a general readership than to Mailer scholars, for whom it presents somewhat less new information. Rollyson draws extensively from Mills and Manso and from interviews in Lennon's *Conversations*, adding some information from his own interviews and research. Similarly, he collates readings of Mailer's works from many of the critical studies discussed above, and in synthesizing these contributes his own. Because Manso's book is limited to transcribed interviews and Mills' offers little literary criticism, Rollyson provides a useful service here, despite an occasional error (e.g., Cherry's hide-away in *An American Dream* is not in Harlem). Although the book presents some harsh judgments of Mailer's personal notoriety, these are tempered by flashes of perceptive praise, as in the recognition that "There is a peculiar integrity to *Maidstone* that is like Mailer's own" (211). In his potentially controversial treatment of his decidedly controversial subject, Rollyson ultimately seeks his own version of the elusive truth.

Michael K. Glenday's *Norman Mailer,* appearing in 1995, briefly enjoyed the advantage of treating the more recent works. Touching on many of the earlier critical and biographical studies, the author suggests new perceptions, occasionally marred by errors of fact: e.g., he refers to Mailer's "first three novels—none of which was written in the first person," when in fact the second and third were first-person narratives; and he calculates that *Ancient Evenings* (1983) was Mailer's "first novel for over twenty-five years," although *Why Are We in Vietnam?* appeared in 1967. Nonetheless, this is a concise and intelligent overview of Mailer's body of work. Ending with a treatment of *Harlot's Ghost*, Glenday hazards the questionable judgment that Mailer's recent work has begun to decline, but concludes that "much more than enough will remain, of a fulfilled bold talent, to stand in high relief amongst the greatest writing of his generation."

Also published in 1995, Joseph Tabbi's *Postmodern Sublime: Technology and American Writing from Mailer to Cyberpunk* is a sophisticated and often arcane study of four major contemporary novelists: Mailer, Thomas Pynchon, Joseph McElroy, and Don DeLillo, and their responses to the growing power of modern technology. Treating such works by Mailer as his infrequently studied *Of a Fire on the Moon*, his seminal and central *An American Dream* and his controversial *Why Are We in Vietnam?*, Tabbi presents new perceptions, some forcefully opinioned, about the complex relationship of Mailer's literary persona to modern scientific phenomena. He then proceeds to the reclusive Pynchon (*Gravity's Rainbow*), McElroy (*Plus*), and DeLillo (*Libra*), suggesting that these writers paradoxically "carry on both the romantic tradition of the sublime and the naturalist ambition of social and scientific realism…in a postmodern culture." This book assumes knowledge of these difficult works and of postmodern literary theory and is therefore somewhat recondite.

In 1999 another biography, *Mailer*, by Mary V. Dearborn, attracted attention. This well-written fourth biography of Mailer is characterized by dramatic strengths and weaknesses. Following Mills, Manso and Rollyson, Dearborn's work enjoys the obvious advantage of presenting more recent material, but also shows assiduous research in incorporating hitherto unpublished information (e.g., Mailer's long-term relationship with Carole Mallory). Dearborn may not be criticized when she dispassionately offers such salacious details, nor condemned for her occasional error of fact (e.g., in Mailer's *An American Dream* [1965] the protagonist, Rojack, does not *stab*, but actually *strangles* his estranged wife, Deborah). More dubious are her continual attempts to second-guess Mailer's personal feelings and motives, as in the case of her flawed perception of his lack of response to the suicide of his friend, Bernard "Buzz" Farbar. If Dearborn's literary criticism of Mailer's works is uneven, it is nonetheless her prerogative to present it; but conjecture about his inner emotions puts her in a less tenable position.

It is fitting and serendipitous that I can end on a highly positive note, with a major event in Mailer scholarship. In 2000, Michael Lennon and Donna Pedro Lennon, noted Mailer experts and his official archivists, published *Norman Mailer: Works and Days*. This impressive volume, more than fifteen years in the making, may well be the most comprehensive bio-bibliography ever compiled on any author. The editors have painstakingly traced and cross-referenced chronologically virtually everything of consequence ever written by Mailer, every interview with him, significant articles, reviews and books about his work, and a plethora of biographical facts and pertinent, incisive quotations from Mailer regarding each of the books in his massive body of work (forty volumes over fifty-two years), from the juvenilia through *The Naked and the Dead* to the landmark anthology *The Time of Our Time* (1998). These are enriched by many excellent photographs of Mailer and his family and friends at various stages of his life, and of the first editions themselves. This exhaustive, meticulous work, with a preface by Mailer, was chosen one of *Choice* magazine's Out-standing Scholarly Titles, and is an indispensable research tool for any student or scholar of Mailer and American literature.

CHAPTER 9

MAILER AND ME

How far back does this go? I was already reading Mailer as a teenager. When I was a sixteen-year-old Ordinary Seaman on the S.S. *John M. Bozeman*, a shipmate recommended *The Naked and the Dead*. My father, particularly impressed by "The Time of Her Time," gave me *Advertisements for Myself*. I still have that beat-up copy, a much-underlined and annotated first edition.

I was living on Charles Street off Greenwich Avenue in the Village, a year out of Columbia, when I read *The Deer Park* and the first version of *An American Dream*, serialized in *Esquire's* first eight issues of 1964. During the 1963-64 academic year, I was 22 years old and holding down what amounted to four jobs: revising and wrapping up my M.A. thesis at Columbia on *The Private Memoirs of Sir Kenelm Digby*; teaching two evening English composition courses at CCNY; taking a 12-hour course load toward the Ph.D. at NYU; and working nights at the *New York Times* credit desk, making decisions on whether to let "business opportunity" ads run without prepayment and taking my break at Gough's, the great, grubby newspaperman's bar across the street, where a draft beer was still 15 cents and you could get a big hamburger with fried onions and French fries for 85 cents. During this time, I wrote my first letter to Mailer. Given the arrogant tone of it, coupled with my knowledge now of what his life was like at age 40, I'm not surprised he never answered. Today, I can be more understanding of his reticence. He tells us much about his perspective at the time in the introduction he wrote eight years later for the 1971 edition of *Deaths for the Ladies (and other disasters)*:

> *Deaths for the Ladies* was written through a period of fifteen months, a time when my life was going through many changes including a short stretch in jail, the abrupt dissolution of one marriage, and the beginning of another. It was also a period in which I wrote very little, and so these poems and short turns of prose were my lonely connection to the one act which gave a sense of self-importance. I was drinking heavily in that period, not explosively as I had at times in the past, but steadily—most nights I went to bed with all the vats loaded, and for the first time, my hangovers in the morning were steeped in dread. Before, I had never felt weak without a drink—now I did. I felt heavy, hard on the first steps of middle age, and in need of a drink. So it occurred to me it was finally not

altogether impossible that I become an alco-
holic. And I hated the thought of that. My
pride and my idea of myself were subject to
slaughter in such a vice.

... I used to wake up in those days...
and the beasts who were ready to root in my
entrails were prowling outside. To a man living on his edge, New York is a jungle...

•

It was not so very funny. In the absence
of a greater faith, a professional keeps himself
in shape by remaining true to his professionalism. Amateurs write when they are drunk.
For a serious writer to do that is equivalent to
a professional football player throwing imagi-
nary passes in traffic when he is bombed, and
smashing his body into parked cars on the
mistaken impression that he is taking out the
linebacker. Such a professional football player
will feel like crying in the morning when he
discovers his ribs are broken.

I would feel like crying too. My pride,
my substance, my capital, was to be found in
my clarity of mind...

And yet Mailer brought himself back from these
depths, and went on to accomplish more in his life and art
than he had before this period of depression. That's why he's a
model for all of us, writers or not: he has personal courage as
well as talent.

I would have had a good deal easier life in academe if

I'd specialized in one of the other authors in whose work I had an intense interest: Shakespeare, say, or Joan Didion, or Emily Dickinson. In 1965, when *An American Dream* was published, any critic could get a license for Mailer-bashing out of a vending machine on any street corner. When *The Armies of the Night* won both the National Book Award and the Pulitzer Prize, *Dream* was suddenly declared a "contemporary classic," not merely by its publisher, but by many literary people who had been reviling it and its author. Yet Mailer could still, as Jimmy Breslin said, "get into trouble in a phone booth." When, in 1971, *The Prisoner of Sex* was published in *Harpers* (precipitating an editorial crisis which ultimately resulted in the resignations of the editor Willie Morris and much of his staff), Mailer again entered the realm of political incorrectness, which he's never really left. The reason is that he's fearless. He says and writes what he wants to, with no regard for consequences.

He was certainly growing larger in my consciousness. During the summer of 1963, I came very close to blows with an anti-Semitic Mailer-reviler at a restaurant, although Mailer certainly didn't need me to defend him. A few years later, after I had taught at the University of Texas at El Paso and become friendly with every bartender in Juarez, I found myself in Athens, Ohio writing a doctoral dissertation on Mailer. I wrote to him again. He remained silent. Prodded once more, he indicated that planned meetings never went well, and that we'd meet spontaneously one day and have a drink, after the dissertation was done.

Well, I tried. In the summer of 1967, I finished the dissertation, got into my Mustang at 3:00 a.m., and drove to Provincetown to find him. Thirty-four years later, after writing *The Structured Vision of Norman Mailer* and innumerable articles and letters, and after many meetings with Mailer, I'm still finding him.

So in late summer 1967, I left Brooklyn at 3:00 AM to visit Mailer spontaneously. Some hours later, with the midmorning sun beating on me and my adrenaline high wearing off, I pulled into the first gas station I saw, jumped out and started asking everybody, "Where's Norman Mailer?" Most bystanders looked at me blankly. Finally, one of the station attendants asked, "You mean that crazy writer fellow from New York?" and told me to drive down Commercial Street until I saw a white Corvette with New York plates. I ran back to my car, only to see the car he'd described pulling into the Howard Johnson's lot. It was jammed with kids, like a clown's circus car, and I astutely noted that the driver wasn't Mailer but a young woman, perhaps eighteen years old. Conscious of the potential ironies of conclusion-jumping, I asked: "Do you happen to know the whereabouts of the famous writer, Norman Mailer?" Everybody laughed.

Reassured, I continued: "You're his kids, right?"

"No, I'm his secretary. *These* are his kids."

Mailer was away at a writers' conference. So much for spontaneity. So I followed the group into the restaurant (this was before the advent of anti-stalking laws), ordered the cheapest thing on the menu (French fries) and learned that despite my perception of myself as the foremost fan and expert on Mailer, I was still a jerk to everyone else.

Well, here I was, in my self-styled role as the primary devotee of (if not authority on) Mailer's works, and I'm told by this officious eighteen-year-old woman, just out of her freshman year at Berkeley, whose job was babysitting and typing an occasional letter, that if I were to return on another occasion and approach the back door I might get a book signed. Not only that, but the advance copies of *Why Are We in Vietnam?* were in at the Provincetown bookstore. So I slipped away, spent my remaining gas and food money on a first edition of *Vietnam* (almost a decade between *The Deer Park* and *An American Dream*, and now here's another novel barely two years after *Dream*), drove back to Brooklyn (the last few miles on fumes) and wrote another chapter.

In early 1968, Mailer read excerpts from the forthcoming *Armies of the Night* at Wesleyan. By now the dissertation was finished; I was a Ph.D., living and teaching in Connecticut. I drove over to Wesleyan and as he walked down the aisle to the stage, handed him a copy of the manuscript. I could see him leafing through it as others spoke. After his reading, I stood at the periphery of a group of academic questioners, not too unobtrusive in my jeans and cowboy boots. Finally, he looked me full in the eyes and said, "Do you have a question, or are you just gonna stand there?"

I didn't want to give him a bag of shit; I just wanted to shake his hand.

So I stepped forward and said, "I don't want to give you a bag of shit. I just want to shake your hand."

He looked at me more penetratingly. "What's your name?"

I told him.

"Did you write this?"

I admitted it.

"Let me borrow it for a month or so, okay? You seem to be the only guy who knows what I'm up to in *An American Dream*."

Subsequently, Mailer sent the manuscript back with

some gracious comments. Among other things, he wrote:

> I...did think your stuff on *The Naked and the Dead* was the best and most interesting criticism that I've read on the book and in fact gave me the desire to go back and read it again.... And your stuff on *An American Dream* was generally very good. If the rest of the book is up to what I saw you've not only a good thesis, but an exciting career ahead as a critic if that should continue to interest you (30 July 1968).

In 1970, we met briefly under similar circumstances, again at Wesleyan. By now I had expanded the dissertation and published *The Structured Vision of Norman Mailer*. I had married, fathered my first daughter, Brett Ashley (Buffy) Leeds, bought a house in the woods and refined my view of myself as iconoclast: the Jeremiah Johnson of academe.

In the 1970s, satires of Mailer in the popular press had become quite broad. For example, the May 1972 issue of *National Lampoon* included a four-page comic book written by Sean Kelly and drawn by Barry Smith entitled *Norman the Barbarian*, in which a caricature of Mailer, dressed in a fur loincloth, armed with a pen and accompanied by a sidekick named Bress-Lin, fights the forces of women's liberation amazons and conquers the Bitch-Goddess Media.

In 1972, the poet and translator Al Poulin called me from SUNY Brockport and told me that Mailer would be speaking in Rochester. He asked if I could arrange to have him drive over to Brockport where I could interview him on TV tape for the Brockport Writers Forum. I wrote Mailer a registered letter, and a few days later the phone rang. Robin, my wife, smiled and said, "Somebody named Norman wants to talk to you."

"Hey, Barry," he said, as though I'd seen him yesterday, "I'm in Boston. I'll be in Rochester in two days. Here's what we'll do. You come to the lecture. Have a car outside. After the question period, we'll drive over to Brockport, have a couple of drinks, and tape the interview. We should be able to do it in under two hours. Tell them to expect us about 2:00 a.m."

Was I excited? Yes. Did the SUNY guys come through? No. Too many problems with getting the studio at that hour, and other logistics. I called Mailer and told him their alternate offer: come next year, and they'd have a Mailer weekend: lecture, parties, a screening of *Maidstone*, and our interview. When I told Mailer, he said okay, but the spontaneous plan would've been better.

One last thing: "If we do it, there's one condition." I waited: what? Belly dancers? Irish coffee? Rocky and Bullwinkle as warm-up?

"You're the only guy I'll do the interview with." That was fine with me, but that gig didn't come about. Al Poulin became seriously ill, and Mailer and I drifted out of even this tangential connection. It would be 1987 before I'd get to interview him (no TV), and in the same season I would be interviewed on TV for the Brockport Writers Forum by my friend, the poet Tony Piccione, largely about the work of Mailer and Kesey.

So we said goodbye on the phone. "Goodbye, Barry."
I was so cool: "Goodbye, Nuh, Nuh, Nuh, NORMAN!"

• • •

More time passed. I went through my own creative crisis, wrote my own deservedly unpublished novel, and turned to the works of other novelists in my critical writings. I taught my 12-hour load year after year, moved up to full professor, and most important, Robin and I had our second daughter, Leslie. In 1981, with my book on Ken Kesey about to be published, I was at an academic conference to speak on Kesey when Michael Lennon, a fellow Mailerian who was to become a good friend, introduced himself and asked why Norman never heard from me anymore. (You don't write; you don't call!) I was surprised: I'd never wanted to make my career by bothering any author, especially Mailer, who I knew guarded his time and privacy.

I wrote him again, we resumed our correspondence, and a series of gradually more personal meetings ensued. On November 8, 1982, he spoke at Yale. After his talk, I approached him. He greeted me warmly and invited me to a party at the apartment of Shelley Fisher Fishkin, then teaching and working on her dissertation at Yale. We had a fine, intense talk, then left for another party, accompanied by Robin and by Dominique Malaquais, the undergraduate daughter of Mailer's friend, Jean Malaquais. We found ourselves wandering through the campus and streets of New Haven with glasses in our hands, talking. I remember quoting the wisdom of my maternal grandmother, and telling Norman what a great influence he'd had on my life. I still feel that way.

In September 1985, Mailer participated in a conference at Connecticut College in New London (formerly Connecticut College for Women), a potentially hostile setting. He was received well, both by his fellow panelists and the audience. Again, he was not merely articulate and forceful, but charming and amiable to me.

It was a tough decision for me in 1987, but I decided to undertake another book on Mailer rather than break new ground on Harry Crews or D. Keith Mano or Joseph Wambaugh. I wrote him, asking for an interview. He responded with characteristic grace and generosity, and after several postponements for more important events in his life, notably a trip to Russia, he decided that we should do it right away. I won't be coy and pretend this wasn't a major experience for me. There I was, in the place where he wrote the books that had so dramatically informed my life's vision, talking intensely with Norman for a morning that went by far too fast. You can read the official transcript of it between these covers.

At the first International Hemingway Conference, held at the John F. Kennedy Library in Boston in 1990, Mailer was the keynote speaker. After his talk, I approached to say hello. He was seated next to Jackie Onassis, who held out her hand as if to have her ring kissed. Norman had turned to say something to his wife Norris.

"I'm happy to meet you, Mrs. Onassis," I said, shaking her hand briefly, "but I'm actually here to see Norman." She seemed startled at my preference; but no Secret Service agents roughed me up, and Mailer turned and greeted me warmly.

When I wrote Norman in 1992, he gave me his Provincetown phone number. I called him from the Provincetown Inn, and he invited Robin and me to dinner at Sal's Place with him and his daughter Maggie, who was an undergraduate at Columbia. We had a great time eating, drinking wine, and talking non-stop. Afterwards, we sat around with Jack, the massive-forearmed proprietor, and talked about the old days in Provincetown. I was being good, and resisted the impulse to ask Jack to arm-wrestle. Later, Mailer wrote me: "I still remember the look in your eye when you restrained yourself from asking Jack, the proprietor, to arm-wrestle with you. If I ever had any doubt of the ferocity you contain and have managed to domicile in yourself, it was removed at that point. What a display of character over physical greed and desire" (28 October 1992).

Norman was in a good mood, having finished his book on Picasso that day. After dinner, he drove us all over Provincetown and its environs, pointing out places we should see in daylight, and apologizing for not arranging to go with us the next day. He had to begin editing the Picasso manuscript. At our hotel, Norman got out to say goodbye. We hugged each other, and he said, "See you soon, buddy."

When I got back home, I had occasion to reread *Tough Guys Don't Dance* and screen the movie version for an article I was writing. It was a pleasant jolt to read about and then view the places we'd just been together.

In 1995, I had the fine experience of having dinner at Norman and Norris's house on Commercial Street, with Robin and Norris, Maggie, and my artist/writer/poet daughter Leslie, who had recently graduated from Connecticut College. After dinner, while our wives and daughters chatted, Norman and I sat up late in his bar overlooking the ocean drinking single malt scotch.

When we ran out of time and energy but not talk, and had exhausted the patience of the women, he suggested we meet for breakfast at Michael Shay's restaurant, which has since become one of my favorite Provincetown haunts. I remember that the Mark Fuhrman controversy had just reached its peak in the news that morning, and I suggested that Norman eventually write something on the O. J. Simpson case. Although he felt the subject was virtually mined out, he did finally write the screenplay for a mini-series years later.

In the years since, I have had a recurrent and gathering gratitude that we are unable to see our futures. The last five years of the decade and the century brought great tragedy and travail, as well as new achievement and triumph for me.

When my beloved daughter Leslie died suddenly in 1996, I had no reason or intention to trouble Norman with my personal life, so I didn't write him of this. But my good friend Mike Lennon interceded: when I wrote Michael of Leslie's death, he immediately informed Norman. A day later, an envelope covered with stamps arrived Special Delivery. In it, Norman sent a beautiful, poetic, heartfelt letter of condolence and commiseration. That letter will remain always in a secret compartment of my heart.

Where can I start to write about Leslie? How can it be other than a series of clichés, like those of any other bereaved father? All I can say is that I miss her terribly, profoundly, irrevocably.

The funeral director, a character out of Evelyn Waugh's *The Loved One*, didn't believe the bereaved parents and sister could arrange and speak at the funeral, so he had a minister waiting in the wings. I had my friend Bob Miles standing by to finish my eulogy in case I became unable to continue. But we did it. We made a pact that we would not only try not to break down during our own speeches, but during one another's, so that we wouldn't set off a chain reaction of uncontrollable, wracking tears. Throughout the assembled, there were audible sobs, even among the tough Motor Vehicle guys Robin worked with. But we did it. Here's what I said:

When Leslie was born, after a predawn drive to the hospital on black ice in a vicious February, she ameliorated everything by the radiance of her smile. That face, that Leslie smile, would melt this snow outside and the ice that encases my heart, our hearts, today. Her literary and artistic accomplishments merely echoed the intensity and beauty of her intuitive center, as her lovely face was but an image of her beautiful soul. I won't see her like again.

My Leslie was a mass of engaging, often frustrating, contradictions. Painfully shy in childhood, she was also furiously independent, as when at age two she refused for hours to wear a winter coat in the coldest weather, never admitting to discomfort. She wanted approval; but when she went to receive her Winthrop fellowship (conferring early selection to Phi Beta Kappa), she wore a black leather jacket to the reception. Her response to the dirty looks she got from officials was, "Fuck them. I got the grades!"

That was Leslie. That is Leslie, because she's here in me, and will be until I die. But the world will never be the same again. I don't know why she had to leave us. But as Millay, one of her favorite poets, wrote, "I only know that summer sang in me/ A little while, that in me sings no more."

At the cemetery, we lay Leslie in the frozen ground. Our friend Ross Baiera read one of her favorite Edna St. Vincent Millay poems, ending with "But you were more than young and sweet and fair/ and the long year remembers you," and then led us in the psalm of David. Everyone waited for a cue as to what they should do next.

"Goodbye, Leslie," I said. What more was there to say? Everything. Nothing. And we left. I'm still trying to say goodbye. I know I never will.

•

And now? Now? I still have days when I wander through the empty house, blinded by tears, calling her name aloud. I haven't lost my sanity, just my heart. Nonetheless, I try to remake my new life, a life without Leslie. What life is that? Well, there's one out there, I suppose. Or in here.

I see now that I'm not just badly bruised like Rocky Balboa after his first fight with Apollo Creed. Something's broken inside me that will never heal. Just as Crohn's Disease is not the 24 hour flu or a mere irritable bowel, my condition is chronic, permanent. There may be remissions, but no physician exists who can cure me.

The summer of 1996 found us in no mood to return to Provincetown. Instead, Robin and Buffy and I took a trip to Newport, where we began to understand the statistical dictum that the vast majority of marriages in which a child dies end in divorce. When, in 1997, Robin showed little or no interest in accompanying me to visit the Mailers, I went alone.

By the summer of 1998, with our marriage sadly eroded after more than thirty years, Robin and I separated. On this visit, which had begun to be an annual event, I was accompanied by my long-time friend Beth, with whom friendship had ripened into something more.

During the fall semester of 1998, teaching my course titled "Norman Mailer: Fifty Years of Achievement," I was so impressed by the intense engagement of my students with Norman's work, and the high quality of their midterm exams, that I called him to ask if we could make a group pilgrimage to visit him. Instead, he made me an even better offer: he came to my class, secretly, to avoid crowds. These students were volunteers, not draftees, and it was they and they alone who deserved to benefit from and enjoy his visit. Beth and I picked Norman up at the train station in Hartford, slipped him in and out of my office and my classroom like Zorro or the Scarlet Pimpernel, and had a fine, stimulating discussion with my students, which Norman repeatedly said he enjoyed as well. Beth and I took him to dinner, dropped him off at Wesleyan where we hooked up with much of his family, including Norris, his sister Barbara, and most of his "kids," and declined their invitation to attend the play in which Norris and Norman's youngest son, John Buffalo, was featured. Instead, we kept our promise to meet my students at Tony's Central Pizza, across the street from the CCSU campus, where we found them amidst a forest of beer bottles and pizza crusts, still avidly debriefing each other.

The pilgrimage idea did not, however, die. In October 1999, I took a group of graduate students from my Mailer/ Kesey seminar to Provincetown to meet Mailer and have a three hour seminar in his living room. They were so grateful, excited, dazzled to the point of awe, and so intelligent in their questions, that I realized the experience was analogous to how I would have felt if one of my professors had taken my class to Key West to visit Hemingway at his home. I was very proud of them, and very grateful to Norman.

The year 2000 brought another fine visit. By now, Beth and I had decided that autumn visits were preferable to summer. That fall, despite Norris's cancer (and the consequent surgery, chemotherapy and radiation) and Norman's painful arthritis, they were not merely stoical and self-deprecating about their own travails, but, as always, warm hosts. Over cold vodka and sushi, followed by hearty Russian borscht, we had the pleasure of discussing Norris's fine first novel, *Windchill Summer* (of which I write in Chapter 10), and of having *two* Mailers sign their books for us.

That's only one example of why it's so exciting to work on an author who's still alive and active. It's a dynamic adventure of constant revelation. Most of us who choose to teach literature have embarked on a voyage of self-discovery, seeking to explain ourselves. I've found myself; but I'm still in the process of finding Mailer.

CHAPTER 10

INTO THE MILLENNIUM

As early as 1962, Mailer was studying Picasso's work in depth with a view to writing an extended study of it. *Portrait of Picasso as a Young Man,* an "interpretive biography" (*Picasso* xii), was not, however, to be completed until 1992, and three more years went by while the permissions were cleared for its 1995 publication.

Picasso may resemble no book of Mailer's so much as *Marilyn.* While the reproductions of Picasso's artwork are central, the text is another work of art. Like a fine actor *entering* a role, Mailer enters another genius's mind: Pablo Picasso's ambition, talent, sexual force. In another way, it reminds one of *Genius and Lust,* so we have a case of "Mailer meets Miller meets Marilyn."

Consider these passages on Picasso's early days in Barcelona:

Picasso's legend would have it that he was an

unusually magnetic personality from early adolescence on, and proved irresistible even then to the prostitutes he visited; before he was sixteen, he would know more about sex, went the legend, than most men will ever know. It was certainly not an image of him that he was about to dispel in later years, but it is not easy to believe (*Picasso* 15).

Further:

Yet if the legend is correct, we are asked to believe that our once-delicate child, dragged daily by the maid to school, has now metamorphosed, just eight years later, into a phenomenally precocious whorehouse stud. Picasso would certainly become the first master of metamorphosis, but it is asking a lot to picture him there ready for action at the age of fourteen or fifteen (16).

Again, Mailer's description of Picasso's relationship with Fernande Olivier is representative of the leap of novelistic imagination that characterizes this biography:

A great deal was obviously shaped in him over those seven years from 1905. Let us enjoy the presence of the number: Fernande was the first of the seven major mistresses and wives who would exercise a measurable influence upon his work. If he has often been depicted as a

monster in his relations with women, let him
also be characterized as wholly magnetized by
such relationships. He would extract a unique
inspiration out of the different style in which
he lived with each woman. And he would
honor each of them in his fashion. Even in
depicting his detestation of his first wife, Olga,
or in the portraits of Dora Maar and his second wife, Jacqueline, which could hardly be
more savage, we can see that he lived, nonetheless, with these women in a manner that
some men never do: He was *in* each relationship—he saw women as his equal. No matter
how hideously he presented these three
women, he could never have delineated them
so if he had not entered into a depth of revul-
sion for what their relationship had become,
and that, in turn, disclosed how hideous were
his own spiritual sores. The physiognomy of
his psyche is present in each of these portray-
als, respectively, of Olga, Dora, and Jacqueline
(94-95).

Here, too, is a good example of how the careful place-
ment of the illustrations (as in *Marilyn*) in close juxtaposition
to Mailer's text enables the book to suggest to the reader the
experience of living in Picasso's mind, for the quotation above
is followed immediately by the artist's portraits of the three
women discussed (95-97).

Yet one more example of Mailer's forceful and incisive
biographical criticism is in order:

Such extremes of cruelty would come later–
by which time (in the late 1920s and 1930s,
and certainly by the 1960s) he was as wealthy
as Midas and profoundly disappointed. He
had taken his long decline down an aesthetic
retreat from the great discoveries between
1907 and 1912. Those had been the five most
creative and astonishing years of his life. But
for the working presence of Georges Braque,
he had been alone, each Cubist painting a re-
connaissance through ambiguities of perception that would have endangered the sanity
of a weaker man. In the face of such inner
peril, this Spaniard, of weak and intermittent
machismo, drenched in his own temerity, full
of sentiments of social and intellectual inferi-
ority, short in stature, was possessed of the
ambition to mine universes of the mind no
one had yet explored (98).

Thus, in his obvious admiration for Picasso, his implicit identification with his sexual habits, his uncompromising critical judgment of the painter's artistic courage in inno-
vation and his eventual compromise, Mailer's work is characterized always by his own unique voice and personal preoccupations.

Again, one realizes that reading one book (or even
several books) by Mailer is an incomplete experience, like
the old folk tale of the blind men and the elephant: One feels
the tail, and says "The elephant is like a rope;" one touches
the trunk and says, "The elephant is like a hose;" one en-
circles a leg, and says, "The elephant is like a tree," and so on

with the tusks, etc.

In 1992 and 1993, Mailer spent six months in Russia, primarily in Minsk, doing research on Lee Harvey Oswald's time there with his wife Marina. Prior to his departure, he wrote me a cryptic letter, suggesting that while his trip to Russia was of undisclosed purpose, given my family's background in law enforcement and his destination (Minsk), I could probably figure out the nature of his mission. Coupled with the exhaustive research Mailer later did in the U.S., including interviews with many of Oswald's associates and few intimates, the finished product, *Oswald's Tale: An American Mystery* (1995) is an unusually original treatment of what had been an already heavily mined vein of historical and literary ore. From his use of detail (e.g., Oswald, without precedent, left his wedding ring, unnoticed by Marina, in a cup on the dresser when he departed for work on the day of John F. Kennedy's assassination) to his penetrating understanding of the mind of Oswald, Mailer's study is unique, forging the skills of the novelist with those of the historian:

> Marina…is now relatively liberated. She no longer needs [Oswald] to survive. We can deduce from the petty tyrannies he has exercised upon her since their marriage just how deep is his lonely and fearful conviction that if she did not need him, she would never have anything to do with him. So his need for love (as opposed to his ability to love) was profound. Love was a safeguard against physically attacking the human species itself. If Kennedy was at the moment the finest specimen of the

American species available, Lee's anxiety over
Marina's love or lack of it was bound to be
large on the night before Kennedy arrived....
No pit was so deep for Oswald as the abyss of
unrequited love (665).

In moving from Oswald to Jesus as his subject, Mailer
went from a small man with a selfish desire for importance,
who achieved notoriety and lasting infamy by killing, and thus
robbing the world of a great man, to a humble man who
achieved true greatness by living modestly and courageously,
selflessly giving his life for the benefit of humanity.

The Gospel According to the Son (1997), too, enters
another's mind, but this time, not that of Marilyn Monroe or
Pablo Picasso, but (gasp) Jesus Christ! This is the operative
definition of *chutzpah*. Yet the narrative voice and rhythms are
convincing in their verisimilitude. There *is* a willing suspension of disbelief. The book has parallels to Mailer's meticulous
research into other cultures (*The Fight*) and historic civiliza-
tions (*Ancient Evenings*).

To me, the most interesting and memorable passage
of the book is Jesus' dialogue with and temptation by Satan.
Christ tells us, "I could also perceive how greed came forth
from his body. For that was kin to the odor that lives between
the buttocks. Therefore I refused his food, but still, the other
odors of his body entered my appetite like the savory that
comes from an oven when food is roasting" (*Gospel* 47). The
image is precise, accurate, evocative, quintessentially Mailer.
The relationship between mood, motive and odor looks back
to *An American Dream,* to *Ancient Evenings*, in fact to his entire
body of work.

Again, Mailer points out (through Satan!) the marginalization of women under the Judeo-Christian tradition. Here, rather than a Devil's advocate, we have the Devil himself accusing God of sexism: "He does not comprehend that women are creatures different from men and live with separate understanding. Indeed, your Father has no inkling of women; His scorn for them is shared by his prophets, who speak, so they claim, with His voice." (50).

And in a passage clearly reminiscent of all the scenes in which a protagonist's courage and virtue is tested against the fear of great height, Jesus is tempted by Satan to jump:

> I felt a temptation to jump.... An abyss was below me. And I knew it would be there for all the generations to come. Whenever they stood on a height, they would live in the wind of that unruly spirit who dwells in our breath and has a terror of the leap. Now the Devil looked at me again with his dark eyes, and the points of light within were like a night of stars; those eyes would promise glory.... If I jumped, the Devil would possess me. I would have leaped to my death at his bidding (54).

This is evocative of *Harlot's Ghost*, of *Tough Guys Don't Dance*, and particularly of Rojack's impulse to jump from the parapet at the beginning of *An American Dream*.

But the most impressive passages in *The Gospel According to the Son* occur in the last few pages of the final chapter, in which Jesus speaks of what has occurred since his resurrection and ascension:

God and Mammon still grapple for the hearts
of all men and all women. As yet, since the
contest remains so equal, neither the Lord nor
Satan can triumph. I remain on the right hand
of God, and look for greater wisdom than I
had before.... My Father, however, does not
often speak to me. Nonetheless, I honor Him.
Surely He sends forth as much love as He can
offer, but His love is not without limit. For
His wars with the Devil grow worse. Great
battles have been lost. In the last century of
this second millennium were holocausts, con-
flagrations, and plagues worse than any that
had come before (240).

Further:

Thereby, let it be understood: My Father may
not have vanquished the Devil. Less than forty
years after I died on the cross, a million Jews
were killed in a war against Rome. The Great
Temple was left with no more than one wall.
Still, the Lord proved as cunning as Satan.
Indeed, He understood men and women better than did the Devil.... Thereby does my
Father still find much purpose for me. It is
even by way of my blessing that the Lord sends
what love He can muster down to that creature who is man and that other creature who
is woman, and I try to remain the source of

love that is tender (241).

The crucial point that I would emphasize here is that Mailer's vision of the cosmos differs in one significant point from that of the Judeo-Christian tradition. This is his consistently stated view in, for example, *An American Dream*, that God cannot be both omnipotent and all good, and that it is a more tenable position to view God and the Devil, good and evil, as locked in a constant struggle for the souls of man and woman. This is, as I have frequently stated, an essentially Manichaean vision, the dualistic religious philosophy of the Persian prophet Manes which teaches that God and the Devil, of comparable strength, are reinforced or weakened by the moral choices of human beings.

In 1998, Mailer published a painstaking selection of his vast writings: the 1277-page retrospective, *The Time of Our Time,* on the fiftieth anniversary of the publication of *The Naked and the Dead.*

The structure of this collection is unique. The selections are not arranged chronologically in the order they were published as might have been expected, but in the order of the time in which they are set. Thus, two passages from *The Naked and the Dead* (1948) bracket the first section of *An American Dream* (1965) in sections entitled "THE SECOND WORLD WAR—I, II and III."

In this work, Mailer succeeds in his intent to represent a history of our century from his peculiarly American viewpoint. But there are additional bonuses. The only substantive new passage, a striking one, is his first direct treatment in print of the 1960 stabbing of his second wife, Adele Morales, in a section titled "The Shadow of the Crime: A Word from the Author." Without evasion or excuse, with consummate dignity, Mailer addresses the notorious incident thus:

> In November 1960, I stabbed my wife Adele with a pen-knife. The surgeons, looking to stanch the internal bleeding, made an incision from the sternum to the pelvis that left her permanently scarred.
>
> Through the years a shadow of the crime would accompany many hours. I could never write about it. Not all woe is kin to prose. It was one matter to be guilty—by inner measure, irredeemably guilty—it was another to present some literary manifest of what was lost and what was wasted, what was given to remorse and what was finally resistant to remorse. Violence is the child of the iron in one's heart, and decomposes by its own laws.
>
> In any event, the marriage was lost.... The damage to our two daughters would be incalculable.... Guilt fed the shadow of the crime.
>
> ...an act of violence is not only a deed but the echo and the shadow of all the voices and all the acts that do not take place and now never will. That is why murder and its sibling, assault, are the most wanton of crimes, for they mangle the possibilities and expectations open to others (*Time* 384-85).

This forceful, uncompromising candor is indicative of

the cumulative value of Mailer's mature vision and hard-won wisdom as expressed in his vast body of work and illuminated in *The Time of Our Time*. We see no slouching, rough beast here. Instead, we watch as this man, this artist, this colossus, strides purposefully and inexorably into the millennium.

Addendum

Windchill Summer **by Norris Church Mailer**

Norris Church Mailer added to her demonstrated talents as teacher, model, actress and artist, that of novelist, when she published her fine first book, *Windchill Summer* (2000). In this, she showed great confidence and courage on several levels. It is impossible to estimate the pressure upon someone writing her first novel in the same house as her Pulitzer-Prize-winning husband of twenty-five years and forty books.

The book itself is rooted in such literary antecedents as *As I Lay Dying* (in terms of shifting, multiple points of view), *The Scarlet Letter* (a guilt-ridden clergyman takes responsibility for his illegitimate paternity), even *The Catcher in the Rye* (in the authenticity of the first person narrative voice of the protagonist). Further, it is a murder mystery replete with red herrings.

More significant is the fact that the novel is a daring exercise in pushing the limits of incorporating real-life characters into fiction, like E. L. Doctorow in such novels as *Ragtime*, or Norman Mailer in such novels as *Harlot's Ghost*. Specifically, Norris Mailer is defiantly bold enough to make two of her principal characters participants in the My Lai massacre: not a "My Lai-like" event, but the actual killings, with the presence of Lieutenant Calley, Captain Medina, and the heroic helicopter pilot, Hugh Thompson, who stopped Calley at gunpoint in mid-massacre. As she told me, she had to fight her editor on this point of authenticity (Norris Church Mailer in conversation, October 7, 2000).

This coming of age novel, set in Arkansas in the 1960s, but with "no mention of Bill Clinton and no autobiography," (NCM) coincidentally features as its protagonist a twenty-one-year-old woman named Cherry. Another interesting parallel to Norman's work is Cherry's independently realized conclusion that God cannot be both omnipotent and all good:

> In fact, it was getting harder as I got older to figure out the whole business of what God does control. I am almost scared to say it out loud, but it seems to me like either God is all-powerful or He is all good, but He can't be both. You know what I mean? How can He really be omniscient and omnipotent, like they teach us in church, and still let things happen like Carlene getting murdered or babies getting cancer or all those Jews getting killed by the Nazis? Is it the Devil that causes all of it? If God could stop it but allows it to happen, then maybe He is not all that caring about us (*Windchill* 104).

This passage of incipient Manichaeism is disarmingly explained by Norris in that the Mailers do see eye to eye on some philosophical issues.

Windchill Summer may not be *The Naked and the Dead*, but it is one hell of a novelistic debut.

In October 2000, after my second reading of *Windchill Summer,* I sat at the Mailers' table and while Norman and Beth looked on, told Norris in detail what I liked about the book.

She thanked me, then flashed a puckish grin and asked, "What if you *didn't* like it, Barry?"

I looked into her eyes. "Is the question, would I perjure myself about literature to please a friend?"

She nodded.

"Never."

That's my final word.

WORKS CITED

Abbott, Jack Henry. *In the Belly of the Beast*. New York: Random, 1981.

Adams, Laura, ed. *Existential Battles: The Growth of Norman Mailer*. Athens: Ohio UP, 1976.

-----. *Will the Real Norman Mailer Please Stand Up*. Port Washington: Kennikat, 1974.

Baldwin, James. *Another Country*. New York: Dial, 1962. New York: Dell, 1963.

Begiebing, Robert J. *Acts of Regeneration: Allegory and Archetype in the Works of Norman Mailer*. Columbia: U of Missouri P, 1980.

-----. *Toward a New Synthesis*. Ann Arbor: UMI Research, 1989.

Bowden, Mark. "Norman Mailer: The Prisoner of Celebrity." *Philadelphia Inquirer Sunday Magazine* 2 Dec. 1984: 40-44.

Braudy, Leo, ed. *Norman Mailer: A Collection of Critical Essays*. Englewood Cliffs: Prentice, 1972.

Bufithis, Philip H. *Norman Mailer*. New York: Ungar, 1978.

Carroll, Paul. "*Playboy* Interview: Norman Mailer." *Playboy* Jan.,1968: 69-72, 74, 76, 78, 80, 82-84. Rpt. in Robert F. Lucid, ed., *Norman Mailer: The Man and His Work*, Toronto: Little, 1971.

Cohen, Sandy. *Norman Mailer's Novels*. Atlantic Highlands: Humanities, 1979.

Dearborn, Mary V. *Mailer*. New York: Houghton Mifflin, 1999.

Des Pres, Terence. Review of *In the Belly of the Beast* by Jack Henry Abbott. *New York Times Book Review*. 18 Jul. 1981: 1.

Didion, Joan. Review of *The Executioner's Song* by Norman Mailer. *New York Times Book Review*. 7 Oct. 1979: 1.

Ehrlich, Robert. *Norman Mailer: The Radical as Hipster*. Metuchen: Scarecrow, 1978.

Flaherty, Joe. *Managing Mailer*. New York: Coward-McCann, 1969.

Foster, Richard. *Norman Mailer*. Minneapolis: U of Minnesota P, 1968.

Glenday, Michael K. *Norman Mailer*. New York: St. Martin's, 1995.

Godden, Richard. *Fictions of Capital: The American Novel from James to Mailer*. Cambridge: Cambridge UP, 1990.

Gordon, Andrew. *An American Dreamer: A Psychoanalytic Study of the Fiction of Norman Mailer*. Rutherford: Fairleigh Dickinson UP, 1980.

Greer, Germaine. *The Female Eunuch*. New York: McGraw-Hill, 1971.

Gutman, Stanley T. *Mankind in Barbary: The Individual and Society in the Novels of Norman Mailer*. Hanover: UP of New England, 1975.

Harmetz, Aljean. "Tracy Wynn Fighting to Get TV-Series Credit." *New York Times* 15 Jan. 1982: C8.

Hemingway, Ernest. *The Garden of Eden*. New York: Scribner's, 1986.

Hershey, Lenore. "Editor's Diary: Mailer and Marilyn," *Ladies Home Journal*, Sept. 1980: 2.

Huxley, Aldous. *Brave New World*. 1932. New York: Harper, 1960.

Kaufmann, Donald L. *Norman Mailer: The Countdown (The First*

Twenty Years). Carbondale: Southern Illinois UP, 1969.

Kelly, Mary Pat. *Martin Scorsese: A Journey*. New York: Thunder's Mouth, 1991.

Kesey, Ken. *One Flew over the Cuckoo's Nest*. New York: Viking, 1962.

Leeds, Barry H. "A Conversation with Norman Mailer." *Connecticut Review*. 10.2 (1988): 1-15. Rpt. in J. Michael Lennon, ed., *Conversations With Norman Mailer*. Jackson: UP of Mississippi, 1988. 359-377.

-----. *The Structured Vision of Norman Mailer*. New York: New York UP, 1969.

Leigh, Nigel. *Radical Fictions and the Novels of Norman Mailer*. New York: St. Martin's, 1990.

Lennon, J. Michael, ed. *Conversations with Norman Mailer*. Jackson: UP of Mississippi, 1988.

-----. *Critical Essays on Norman Mailer*. Boston: Hall, 1986.

-----. "Mailer's Radical Bridge." *Narrative,* 7 (Fall 1977): 170-88.

-----. *Norman Mailer: Works and Days*. Shavertown, Pennsylvania: Sligo Press, 2000 (with Donna Pedro Lennon).

Lucid, Robert F., ed. *Norman Mailer: The Man and His Work*. Toronto: Little, 1971.

Lupack, Barbara Tepa, ed. *Take Two: Adapting the Contemporary American Novel to Film*. Bowling Green: Bowling Green State U Popular P, 1994.

Mailer, Norman. *Advertisements for Myself*. New York: Putnam's, 1959.

-----. *An American Dream*. New York: Dial, 1965.

-----. *Ancient Evenings*. Boston: Little, 1983.

-----. "An Appreciation of Cassius Clay." *Partisan Review* Summer 1967. Rpt. in *Existential Errands*. Boston: Little, 1972. 264.

-----. *The Armies of the Night*. New York: NAL, 1968.

-----. *Barbary Shore*. New York: Rinehart, 1951.

-----. "The Best Move Lies Very Close to the Worst." *Esquire* October 1993: 60-64. Rpt. in *The Time of Our Time*. New York: Random House, 1998.

-----. *Cannibals and Christians*. New York: Dial, 1966.

-----. "Death." *The Presidential Papers*. New York: Putnam's, 1963. 213-67.

-----. *Deaths for the Ladies (and other disasters)*. New York: Putnam's, 1962. New York: NAL, 1971.

-----. *The Deer Park*. New York: Putnam's, 1955.

-----. *The Executioner's Song*. New York: Warner, 1979.

-----. *Existential Errands*. Boston: Little, 1972.

-----. *The Fight*. Boston: Little, 1975.

-----. "Fury, Fear, Philosophy: Understanding Mike Tyson." *Spin* Sept. 1988: 40-44, 78.

-----. *The Gospel According to the Son*. New York: Random, 1997.

-----. *Genius and Lust*. New York: Grove, 1976.

-----. *Harlot's Ghost*. New York: Random, 1991.

-----. "King of the Hill." *Life* 19 March 1971: 18F-36. Rpt. as *King of the Hill*. New York: NAL, 1971. Rpt. in *Existential Errands*. 3-36.

-----. *King of the Hill*. New York: NAL, 1971.

-----. Letter to the author. 30 July 1968.

-----. Letter to the author. 28 October 1992.

-----. *Maidstone: A Mystery*. New York: NAL, 1971.

-----. *Marilyn*. New York: Grosset & Dunlap, 1973.

-----. *Miami and the Siege of Chicago*. New York: NAL, 1968.

-----. *The Naked and the Dead*. New York: Rinehart, 1948.

-----. *Of a Fire on the Moon*. Boston: Little, Brown, 1971.

-----. *Of Women and Their Elegance*. New York: Simon and Schuster, 1980.

-----. *Oswald's Tale: An American Mystery*. New York: Random, 1995.

-----. *Portrait of Picasso as a Young Man*. New York: Atlantic Monthly Press, 1995.

-----. *The Presidential Papers*. New York: Putnam's, 1963.

-----. *The Prisoner of Sex*. Boston: Little, Brown, 1971.

-----. *St. George and the Godfather*. New York: NAL, 1972.

-----. *Some Honorable Men*. Boston: Little, 1976.

-----. "Strawhead." *Vanity Fair* April 1986: 58-67.

-----. "The Time of Her Time." *Advertisements for Myself*. New York: Putnam's, 1959. 478-503.

-----. *The Time of Our Time*. New York: Random, 1998.

-----. *Tough Guys Don't Dance*. New York: Random, 1984.

-----. *A Transit to Narcissus*. Introduction. By Mailer. New York: Fertig, 1978. vii-x.

-----. "The White Negro." *Advertisements for Myself*. New York: Putnam's, 1959. 337-358.

-----. *Why Are We in Vietnam?* New York: Putnam's, 1967.

Mailer, Norris. *Windchill Summer.* New York: Random, 2000.

Manso, Peter. *Mailer: His Life and Times*. New York: Simon, 1985.

McConnell, Frank D. *Four Postwar American Novelists*. Chicago: U of Chicago P, 1977.

Merrill, Robert. *Norman Mailer*. Boston: Twayne, 1978.

-----. *Norman Mailer Revisited*. New York: Twayne, 1992.

Millett, Kate. *Sexual Politics*. New York: Doubleday, 1970.

Mills, Hilary. *Mailer: A Biography*. New York: Empire, 1982.

Orlando Sun-Sentinel 16 November 1988: 1E.

Parker, Hershel. *Flawed Texts and Verbal Icons: Literary Authority in American Fiction*. Illinois: Northwestern UP, 1984.

Peary, Gerald. "Medium-Boiled Mailer." *Sight and Sound International Film Quarterly* Spring 1987: 104-7.

Poirier, Richard. *Norman Mailer*. New York: Viking, 1972.

Radford, Jean. *Norman Mailer: A Critical Study*. New York: Harper, 1975.

Review of *Deaths for the Ladies (and other disasters)*. *Time* 30 March 1962: 84.

Rollyson, Carl. *The Lives of Norman Mailer: A Biography*. New York: Paragon, 1991.

Sciolino, Elaine. "Mailer Visits C.I.A. and Finds He's in Friendly Territory. Really." *New York Times* 2 Feb. 1992.

Scorsese, Martin, dir. *Raging Bull*. United Artists, 1980.

Smith, Dinitia. "Tough Guys Make Movie." *New York* 12 Jan. 1987: 32-35.

Solotaroff, Robert. *Down Mailer's Way*. Urbana: U of Illinois P, 1974.

Tabbi, Joseph. *Postmodern Sublime: Technology and American Writing from Mailer to Cyberpunk*. Cornell, 1995.

Wenke, Joseph. *Mailer's America*. Hanover: UP of New England, 1987.

Winters, Shelley. *Shelley II: The Middle of My Century*. New York: Simon and Schuster, 1989.

INDEX

Other books from
Pleasure Boat Studio: A Literary Press

Fiction
Another Life and Other Stories, by Edwin Weihe
If You Were With Me Everything Would Be All Right,
stories by Ken Harvey
In Memory of Hawks, and Other Stories from Alaska,
by Irving Warner
Pronoun Music, stories by Richard Cohen
Setting Out: The Education of Li-li, a novel by Tung Nien,
translated from the Chinese by Mike O'Connor
The Eighth Day of the Week, a novel by Alfred Kessler

Poetry
Women in the Garden, by Mary Lou Sanelli
In Blue Mountain Dusk, by Tim McNulty. A Broken Moon book
Lineage, by Mary Lou Sanelli. An Empty Bowl book
Nature Lovers, by Charles Potts
Original Sin, by Michael Daley. Chapbook
P'u Ming's Oxherding Tales, by P'u Ming, translated from the
Chinese by Red Pine. An Empty Bowl book
Saying the Necessary, by Edward Harkness
The Basin: Life in a Chinese Province,
by Mike O'Connor. An Empty Bowl book
The Light on Our Faces: A Therapy Dialogue,
by Lee Miriam Whitman-Raymond. Chapbook
The Politics of My Heart, by William Slaughter
The Rainshadow, by Mike O'Connor. An Empty Bowl book
The Rape Poems, by Frances Driscoll
The Straits, by Michael Daley. An Empty Bowl book
Too Small to Hold You, by Kate Reavey. Chapbook
Untold Stories, by William Slaughter. An Empty Bowl book

Essays
The Handful of Seeds: Three and a Half Essays,
by Andrew Schelling. Chapbook
When History Enters the House: Essays from Central Europe,
by Michael Blumenthal

Pleasure Boat Studio: A Literary Press
8630 Wardwell Road
Bainbridge Island•WA 98110-1589 USA
Tel/Fax: 888.810.5308
URL: www.pbstudio.com

from
Pleasure Boat Studio

an essay written by Ouyang Xiu,
Song Dynasty poet, essayist, and scholar,
on the twelfth day of the twelfth month
in the renwu year (January 25, 1043)

I have heard of men of antiquity who fled from the world to distant rivers and lakes and refused to their dying day to return. They must have found some source of pleasure there. If one is not anxious for profit, even at the risk of danger, or is not convicted of a crime and forced to embark; rather, if one has a favorable breeze and gentle seas and is able to rest comfortably on a pillow and mat, sailing several hundred miles in a single day, then is boat travel not enjoyable? Of course, I have no time for such diversions. But since 'pleasure boat' is the designation of boats used for such pastimes, I have now adopted it as the name of my studio. Is there anything wrong with that?

Translated by Ronald Egan
The Literary Works of Ou-yang Hsiu
Cambridge University Press

Norman Mailer with Barry Leeds

About the Author

Barry H. Leeds, CSU Distinguished Professor of English at Central Connecticut State University, is the author of three books: *The Structured Vision of Norman Mailer, Ken Kesey,* and *The Enduring Vision of Norman Mailer,* and of over two hundred articles, reviews, and anthology chapters. He received his B.A. (1962) and M.A. (1963) degrees from Columbia, and his Ph.D. from Ohio University (1967). Dr. Leeds has taught at CCSU since January 1968, and prior to that at the City University of New York, the University of Texas at El Paso, and Ohio University (Athens). He has lectured at universities and conferences nationwide and internationally, and has been interviewed in a variety of media: television, radio, and newspapers. He was Editor-in Chief of *Connecticut Review* from 1989 to 1992, and a member of the Editorial Board from 1986 to 1995. Dr. Leeds has served as a consultant to various university presses, administrations, and organizations such as the Association of American Medical Colleges. He is listed in *Who's Who in America* and over a dozen other such directories. Initially a Shakespearean, then a specialist in Seventeenth Century metaphysical poetry, Leeds has for many years devoted himself to studying the ongoing work of contemporary American authors who are not conveniently dead, with their body of work closed. Thus, his writing, like theirs, is always a work in progress.

Photo by Norris Church Mailer